NEW

ENGLISH

INTERIORS

NEW

ELIZABETH METCALFE
PHOTOGRAPHY BY DEAN HEARNE

ENGLISH

AT HOME
WITH TODAY'S
CREATIVES

F FRANCES
LINCOLN

INTERIORS

INTRODUCTION

The English style of decorating is synonymous with colour, pattern and a certain eccentricity. At its best, it is deeply personal, telling the stories of those who inhabit the space, as much as it offers a visual feast. But there was a time, back in the 1990s and 2000s, when English decoration took a rather less lively turn and centred around a palette of beiges, greys and all the nondescripts in between. Some heralded it 'modern English style', but in its uniformity it said very little of the individual who lived there.

Thankfully, interiors filled with colour, life and objects are very much back. Whether we see that as proof that the bold English decorating spirit still reigns strong or as a reaction against the uncertain times we live in, it is a style defined by layers, with the owner's personality intricately woven throughout. This book is about just that: it is a celebration of today's most exciting creatives, across 22 homes that embrace colour and pattern in their infinite variety. Ranging from interior designers and illustrators to artists and antique dealers, some of the homes started off rather more grey – architect George Saumarez Smith's house in Winchester (pp.46–55) took over a decade to gain its more colourful layers – while others have always been brimful of pattern-rich wallpapers and bold colours. For some, such as the artist Annie Morris (pp.32–45), and fashion stylist and designer Lucinda Chambers (pp.68–77), colour is a fundamental part of their lives, and their homes are an extension of that.

More than a handful of those featured here cite the work of John Fowler, the iconic twentieth-century decorator, and David Hicks, the renowned designer and colourist, among their inspirations. Their influence is obvious, with wallpapers, fabrics, charming details and lovingly collected objects among new English interiors' defining characteristics. More recently, we have visionary architectural and interior designer Ben Pentreath among those we can thank for the resurgence of colour and pattern in our homes. A superb blend of present and past, the spaces he creates resist fads, put comfort first, and are rich with joyous colour and character.

Here, there are houses that are punchy and bold in their decoration, such as creative consultant Max Hurd's brilliantly offbeat house in north-west London (pp.100–111, where its clashing colours, patterns and imaginative details have a theatrical quality. But there are also houses at the earthier end of the spectrum, such as illustrator Fee Greening's idyllic cottage in Dorset (pp.196–207), which has a deeply comforting, homespun quality. So too does the softly coloured East Sussex home of Tess and Alfred Newall (pp.56–67), the decorative artist and furniture maker duo, where the palette is rooted in the natural world and almost everything is the work of their own hands. And while this is a world away from the bolder, jewel-like palettes of, say, Ariadne and Olympia Irving's flat in north London (pp.10–21), there is one thing that unites them: they are visual moodboards

6

'THE BEST ROOMS HAVE SOMETHING TO SAY ABOUT THE PEOPLE WHO LIVE IN THEM.'
David Hicks

for their owners, overflowing with personality. Some provide a canvas on which to experiment; some are a place where their owners' favourite colours and fabrics come together in joyful abandon. In fact, you may even find a sprinkling of grey and a fair few white walls in the mix: sometimes this provides a pause from more riotous elements, or in the case of the all-white walls at gallerist and interior designer Tobias Vernon's cottage (pp.164–173), they create an environment in which colourful objects and paintings can really sing.

For a book titled *New English Interiors*, it might seem odd that many of those featured have been 20 or more years in the making. Interior decorator Gavin Houghton's house in south London (pp.184–195), has offered a playful take on country-house style for well over a decade. Some, including interior decorator Mary Graham's house in North Yorkshire (pp.154–163) and designer Holly Howe's end-of-terrace in north London (pp.90–99), have taken shape in the past few years. Whether created over a lifetime or more recently, these joyful, uplifting, keenly individual interiors speak of today. They are not about rip-out culture, nor do they constitute a flash-in-the-pan style that bows to trends or can be achieved instantly. Rather, this is a style that improves with age and benefits from its layers being allowed to evolve gently. Interior decorator Carlos Garcia (pp.228–239) terms it 'slow decoration'. Even in those interiors that have been pulled together more recently, there is a sense that the contents have been gathered slowly and reflect a taste that is ever-evolving.

That is a common theme between all of the houses here: none of them are fixed in aspic. Some are very much works in progress, such as Jorge Perez-Martin and David Gibson's handsome limestone villa near Stroud (pp.144–153), where the decoration has been thoughtfully evolving for eight or so years (and could well continue for another eight). Fee's house is also still very much gaining its layers: a new bedroom and bathroom are on the cards when funds allow. But few of the houses featured in this book – even those that seem pulled together perfectly – will ever be seen by their owners as 'finished', and that is the joy of them. Almost all of the interiors are borne out of a love for collecting – everything from furniture and art to curious flea-market finds and ceramics – and, as a consequence, they continue to shift and evolve. Perhaps, 'accumulating' is a better word: for these interiors aren't necessarily based around prestigious art collections, but more an appreciation for things – whether they cost £1 or £1,000 – that are beautiful or intriguing.

All of the houses featured do indeed make a pretty picture, but they are not interiors solely created with an Instagram shot in mind. What became clear when we photographed them is that they all – in their own particular way – have one elusive quality: they are rich with feeling and mood. They also all prioritise comfort, providing environments that offer security and nourish the souls of those who live in them. Ranging from small London flats and country cottages, to sprawling estates and large townhouses, I hope that they might provide inspiration on how to live with layers of glorious colour, pattern and objects. Equally, I hope they might also give us the confidence to let our personalities – with their many facets and quirks – guide how we decorate our homes.

OLYMPIA & ARIADNE IRVING

Homeware designers, north London

Sisters Ariadne and Olympia Irving grew up surrounded by good taste and layers of bohemian loveliness. Their mother is the globetrotting textile designer Carolina Irving, while their father, Ian Irving, is a prominent silver and art dealer. Home, for a good portion of their lives, was a spectacular textile-laden apartment in New York, which proved to be a particularly formative influence. 'Our parents are our biggest inspiration,' says Ariadne, acknowledging that this is not necessarily the relationship every 30-year-old has with their parents. 'They taught us how to appreciate beautiful things,' explains Olympia, who in 2018, along with her mother and sister, founded Carolina Irving & Daughters, a pattern-rich, craft-led homeware brand. 'There were never any rules in the way they decorated, which gave us so much freedom to work out our own style,' she adds.

And what better place to do that than in the north London flat that the sisters have been renting together since 2020. Having spent a few years living separately in west London, they decided to regroup soon after the first lockdown and relocated to leafy De Beauvoir. 'We quickly realised this would be the dream living and working space for us,' says Olympia, of the three-floor flat, which functions more like a townhouse, with its lovely first-floor sitting room, light-filled conservatory and generous dining room just off the kitchen. 'It felt like a country house in London,' she adds. 'Our brand is all about entertaining, and this seemed like the best place for long lunches and candlelit dinners,' says Olympia. The fact that the owners gave them licence to paint its all-white walls clinched the deal. 'We knew that being able to put colour on the walls would transform it,' explains Ariadne.

The pair spent the best part of a year pondering paint colours. 'We looked at the rooms in the mornings and evenings, and in winter and in summer, to work out what we wanted,' explains Olympia. They already had a good stash of furniture – a mix of colour-packed pieces inherited from their parents and bought at auction – so finding tones that could handle these was also key. 'I mean, for the sitting room it was kind of a question of, what works with a leopard-print chair and a suzani-covered octagonal ottoman?' says Olympia, referring to two of their most cherished possessions, which their father originally bought from Robert Kime in the 1980s. 'We'd never get rid of either of them, and are already bickering about who will get them when we split up,' Ariadne adds, laughing.

Thankfully, choosing paint colours proved a less contentious matter. A cheery yellow – 'Imperial Chinese Yellow' from Papers and Paints – was chosen for the sitting room, while they opted for 'Deep Apple Green', also from Papers and Paints, in the dining room, which gives the space a certain opulence.

The light-filled conservatory off Olympia and Ariadne Irving's kitchen doubles as their studio. The banquette is upholstered in their mother, Carolina Irving Textiles', 'Palermo' fabric in china blue, while the cushions include a 'Checkerboard' design from a collaboration between Carolina Irving & Daughters and Atelier Raff.

'I guess both of the colours keep you cosy in a city that can be grey,' explains Olympia, whose own bedroom is painted in Farrow & Ball's soothing 'Setting Plaster'. The sisters admit they were a bit worried about using punchier tones for the living areas, but as soon as the walls were layered up with textiles and art, their fears were allayed. 'Our dad kept saying that we could always paint it white again if we hated it,' says Ariadne. 'I guess our parents have taught us to be brave.' In her own bedroom, Ariadne opted for a minty green that she softened with recycled chintz curtains and a floral lilac headboard. 'We've got hundreds of photographs from our parents of their old apartments before we were born, and weirdly lots of the colours we've used, like green and lavender, are in those,' she explains. 'The references must be subconsciously lodged in our brains.' Although the girls did not make a particular effort to link the rooms with colour, they sit together beautifully as a whole. 'Everything somehow connects in a way that we hadn't totally foreseen,' says Ariadne, observing how yellows and greens thread throughout.

Undoubtedly, the constraints of the rental pushed Ariadne and Olympia to be more creative. Grey carpets were covered up with inexpensive striped dhurries – blue in the sitting room, yellow in Olympia's room and red in Ariadne's – that were bought via Etsy from Jaipur. Any necessary, but unsightly, elements were imaginatively masked with fabric. The television in the sitting room was hidden behind a pretty cafe curtain ('We whittled it down from about 50 different bits of fabric,' recalls Ariadne), while curtains – fashioned from one of their mother's fabrics and a tablecloth, joined together with fabric tape – were added between the dining room and kitchen to tone down the lurid kitchen lights. 'It took three years of sitting down for supper and being driven mad by the lights for us to finally realise that curtains would solve it,' explains Olympia. In the sitting room, an IKEA sofa was zhuzhed up with a slipcover that the sisters had made from their mother's 'Nino' fabric. 'We like the idea of changing it in the summer,' says Ariadne.

'We didn't want anything to be set in stone and liked the idea of being able to change things up,' her sister adds.

It is remarkable how the flat feels like the result of a lifetime of collecting. Thanks to the hand-me-downs from their parents, it is in part just that, but it has also been artfully layered up by the sisters. Low and high confidently sit side by side, such as in the sitting room, where a set of six eighteenth-century mezzotints hang above a Shell Motor Oil trinket that the girls picked up for a song from Kempton Antiques Market. 'I love knick-knacks like that,' explains Ariadne, whose room is layered up with a collection of framed pressed seaweed samples, starfish and Iznik plates. 'Ariadne is much better than me at fine-tuning,' admits Olympia. Some pieces found particularly good homes, such as a suzani in the sitting room that looks as if it could have been made for the space. 'That's been in our lives since we were four,' recalls Ariadne. Originally, a vast eighteenth-century equestrian portrait was destined for the sitting room, but when they could not squeeze it up the stairs, they decided to put it in the dining room. 'It's a strange piece, with really weird proportions, but it's perfect for that wall there,' says Ariadne.

The house might be a mishmash of pieces, but ultimately what brings it all together is the fact that the sisters are fastidious in their arranging. 'As soon as you start placing things with intention, it stops being clutter,' says Olympia. 'Ariadne spent hours placing the shells on the mantelpiece, which gives order to what otherwise could have been disorder,' she says. The pair are also committed to only buying things that they really love, and they trudge through auctions to find the right pieces. 'They have to be things that we really gravitate to,' says Ariadne. Some are as practical as they are decorative, such as the 3-metre long dining table, which was chosen for the fact it could play host to large lunches and dinners. 'Everything we've done here revolves around the fact that we want this house to be filled with life,' says Olympia. It is a pretty good basis on which to create a home.

The girls settled on 'Imperial Chinese Yellow'
by Papers and Paints for the walls of the
first floor sitting room. This room seamlessly
combines high and low, with a suzani-covered
octagonal ottoman from Robert Kime
(a gift from their father), IKEA's 'Farlov' sofa,
reupholstered in Carolina Irving Textiles'
'Nino' fabric and an elegantly arranged
mishmash of pieces adorning every surface.

The dining room, which is painted in 'Deep Apple Green' from Papers and Paints, features a vast eighteenth-century equestrian portrait, which was bought by the sisters' father and destined for the sitting room before they realised they could not get it up the stairs. The table is covered in an 'Indian Vine' tablecloth in pink by Carolina Irving & Daughters.

Ariadne's bedroom walls are painted in 'Sèvres Green' from Papers and Paints, with an Original Bed Company four-poster that is upholstered in 'Mimosa Vine' from Carolina Irving Textiles. Olympia commissioned ceramicist Katy Stubbs to make the plate for Ariadne's birthday, inspired by her sister's love for Mexican tin decorations, with the central charm depicting the sisters' dog Pepito.

On the top floor, Olympia's bedroom is painted in Farrow & Ball's soothing 'Setting Plaster'. The striped dhurrie rug was bought from Jaipur via Etsy, while the fabric hanging behind the Original Bed Company bed is 'Carnation Stripe' by Carolina Irving Textiles.

BENEDICT FOLEY & DANIEL SLOWIK

Designers and dealers, Essex

Asoulless storage unit or a longer-term countryside rental? Such was the conundrum for designers Benedict Foley and Daniel Slowik nine years ago, when they were contemplating what to do with their combined – and rather hefty – collection of antiques and art. Thankfully, they settled for the latter option, striking out eastwards from Daniel's small flat in London's De Beauvoir on their search for a characterful weekend bolt-hole they could rent. 'This is the first place we saw, and we quickly realised that the only way is, indeed, Essex,' says Benedict, with a wry smile, referring to the pink former millworkers' cottage, down a quiet lane in peak Constable country, next to the River Stour.

Its idyllic setting was a big attraction, but so too was the house's eccentric charm. While the estate agent was a little bemused by this three-bedroom cottage, which has barely changed since it was built in 1804, with its warren of small rooms, original larder, old blue-and-yellow fitted kitchen and rather rudimentary downstairs bathroom, Benedict and Daniel were thrilled. 'We loved that it wasn't a typical rental and hadn't really ever been modified,' says Benedict. Until the 1920s, it had been two cottages – and it still has a narrow staircase at either end of the house, one of which leads directly into Daniel's bedroom and the other to a small corridor. 'It has character in spades, including being self-washing,' Benedict

adds with just a hint of sarcasm, referring to the fact that the cottage often floods when the river levels rise. Thankfully, the pair aren't in the least precious. 'Most bits of antique furniture are on legs, anyway, and we just pop upholstered pieces up on bricks if needs be,' says Benedict.

At its heart, this is a collector's house, where every surface, wall, corridor and unsuspecting corner is filled with delights that range from a small Roman votive carving of Apollo and a bonkers early nineteenth-century porcelain table lamp to an array of occasional tables and majolica pottery. 'It's a real mishmash of pieces that we've collected, bought at auctions or been given over the years,' says Benedict. There were also a few nice enough pieces that came with the house, including the ivy-patterned curtains and William IV cabinet in the dining room, and the wardrobes in Daniel's bedroom. It is exactly the sort of playfully conceived house that you might expect from such a creative duo: Daniel, who launched his eponymous interior design business a few years ago, spent over 25 years working across the antiques and decoration departments at Sibyl Colefax & John Fowler; Benedict, a decorator, dealer and frame-maker, is something of a polymath, who likens his multi-disciplined approach to that of a large-scale collage artist. 'Like with our clients, what we tried to do was find a narrative to build on,' says Benedict.

'The story here was that it belonged to a dowager who had downsized from a bigger house and had lots of large pieces of furniture that needed to be slotted in,' Daniel elaborates.

Slot is certainly the right word, for the cottage presented its fair share of constraints. 'It has its own very peculiar logic and we've not tried to fight that,' Benedict explains. For starters, anything of any size destined for upstairs had to be taken in through the large coffin window in the spare bedroom. And then there is the fact that the couple had rather a lot of doors to contend with: the sitting and dining rooms each have five, some of which were intended to provide millworkers with a view of the boats passing by. This not only gave them fewer walls to put furniture against, but also – rather unfortunately, for a couple with hundreds of works of art between them – limited hanging space. 'We quickly realised that if we didn't put pictures on doors then we'd have barely any space to hang them,' says Daniel. And so, in the dining room, the larder door features a pinboard designed by Benedict, featuring Sibyl Colefax & John Fowler's 'Squiggle' fabric and a frame based on traditional Baltic wooden architecture. The door leading up to Daniel's bedroom features a twentieth-century landscape that Benedict bought him as a present. 'It features an old timber barn along the vale from where we live and I absolutely love it,' says Daniel.

Another challenge came in finding a way to make their stash of furniture work within the modestly proportioned rooms. In the sitting room, two perfectly sized sofas – one that they owned when they first moved in and another covered with a Brussels weave loop that they snapped up at auction more recently – occupy the space perfectly. A japanned Regency tray serves as a coffee table, while a sweet armchair, upholstered in chartreuse 'Irish Linen' that Daniel has designed as part of his new line of fabrics, sits snugly next to the fireplace, without encroaching on the doorway through to the dining room. I get the sense that they rather enjoyed the challenge of piecing it all together. 'It was a case of moving things around to somehow make our lives fit into the cottage,' confirms Daniel. A linen press-turned-bar, papered inside with yet more 'Squiggle' wallpaper, fills the spot behind one of the sofas and sits just millimetres from the ceiling. 'Using over-proportioned furniture in small rooms actually gives the sense that the space is larger,' explains

Daniel. The large nineteenth-century French nocturne hanging above the sofa creates a similar effect. 'It's a funny dark corner and having a moonlit scene there somehow helps,' Benedict explains.

Dark corners aside, this is an interior shaped by colour – from Benedict's lilac granny-chic bedroom to Daniel's elegant bedroom in 'Dix Blue' by Farrow & Ball. 'We liked the idea that the dowager had tricked the cottage up with some fun colours,' explains Benedict. The couple admit they can't take any credit for the kitchen, which remains as they found it, with sunshine yellow walls, cobalt blue units and red floors. 'We actually have no idea what the yellow paint is, so every time a bit peels off from the damp, I just have to stick it back on,' says Benedict. The sitting room glows in Farrow & Ball's 'Wet Sand' after Benedict painted it, with a glass of wine in hand, during lockdown evenings. 'We were getting a bit bored and the great thing about changing the colours is that it allows you to see all of your things afresh,' says Benedict. The bar in the sitting room, for instance, was once white, but now packs a punch in a bold turquoise.

These colours give the cottage a certain energy, but so too does the fact that this is a space in continual flux. 'It's fun to move things to different rooms and we're always tinkering,' says Benedict. 'For me that's what decorating should all be about,' Daniel adds. 'Even for clients, I like schemes to be a little haphazard, and to slowly evolve and gain layers.' Pieces come and go at the cottage with ease. Sometimes new acquisitions prompt Daniel and Benedict to rethink entire rooms, but other pieces gently find their place. A plaster lamp from their friend Viola Lanari, for instance, has found a home on the dresser in the dining room, while one of Jermaine Gallacher's 'Zigzag' tables has proved the perfect accompaniment for the armchair in the sitting room. Benedict's playful creations, which range from frames to ostrich-plume-shaped wall brackets and lion's paw doorstops, also add to the layered mix. Sometimes rooms take on entirely new guises, such as the guest bedroom upstairs, which spent a year as Benedict's studio. Now it is a charming twin, with each bed made up from Daniel's new 'Trellis' fabric in dijon yellow. 'We both don't see this house as really being decorated,' explains Benedict. 'It's fluid rather than static, and that's the fun of it.' I have to agree.

A George III linen-press serves as a bar, papered inside with Sibyl Colefax & John Fowler's 'Squiggle' and painted in a bespoke colour that is a close match to Farrow & Ball's 'Lobster'. The diamond patterned cushion is made from Daniel's 'Trellis' fabric in chartreuse. The dining table is draped in a cloth made from Daniel's 'Ivy Trellis' in cornflower blue, while the dresser behind – which was already there and painted white by Benedict – plays host to a collection of Regency Spode ceramics.

In the little hallway between the kitchen and dining room, bronze green painted walls – 'Pimlico Green' from Sibyl Colefax & John Fowler – bathe a 19th century glazed terracotta Virgin and Child in a rather classical light. Next door, the primary coloured kitchen remains as the couple found it with sunshine yellow walls, cobalt blue units and red floors.

Upstairs, Daniel's room is resplendent in Farrow & Ball's 'Dix Blue', while the bed canopy made from an old curtain, half a table top and Swedish wallpaper was fashioned by Benedict. The colour in Benedict's bedroom – which he calls 'Lilac Wine' – was specially mixed and is topped with a hand-printed Swedish paper border. The chintz quilt is early Victorian.

ANNIE MORRIS & IDRIS KHAN

Artists, West Sussex

Annie Morris and Idris Khan are two of the brightest lights in the contemporary art world. She is best known for her brightly coloured 'Stack' sculptures and surreal oil-stick drawings; Idris, for his large-scale, brooding and – until a recent move towards colour – monochrome works, which combine painting, sculpture and photography, and earned him an OBE in 2017. As people, there is something of their art about them too – Annie is a whirlwind, fizzing with energy, while Idris is more measured and contemplative. And their seventeenth-century weekend house, nestled on a hillside not far from Petworth, in West Sussex, certainly speaks of this dynamic: it brims with colours, patterns, objects and contemporary art, but is underpinned by a distinct calm.

Annie and Idris bought the three-bedroom cottage in 2021, keen for an escape from their busy lives in London, where they live in a Georgian townhouse with their two children. Nothing – not even the fact that Idris couldn't stand up in most of the downstairs rooms – could deter them. 'It's just in such a pretty spot, down a winding track,' explains Annie. 'We put an offer in on my birthday and completed almost two months later, on Annie's birthday,' Idris recalls. They quickly enlisted the help of two long-time collaborators, who had worked on their other houses in France and London – architect Ros Quinn

and interior designer Gavin Houghton. Ros helped them make sense of the space, including digging down in the sitting room and hallway to create extra height, as well as stealing a slither of bedroom upstairs to widen the corridor. 'The changes were subtle, but the idea was to make it feel like it could have always been like this,' says Annie, pointing out the reclaimed Purbeck stone slabs, originally from a sixteenth-century church, that now form the floor in the entrance hallway and kitchen.

To cross the threshold of the cottage is to enter a world full of charm, life and wit. From the joyful cat letter-rack by Annie's friend and mentor, the late artist Ann Stokes, that greets you in the little entrance, to their children's drawings that are tacked up above the kitchen table and the green ceramic poodle that serves as a toothbrush holder in the couple's yellow bathroom, this is an interior that doesn't take itself too seriously. It's joyful and a bit kitsch, pieced together from objects that make the couple smile or hint at a curious backstory. And yet there is a discipline and control that mean the space never becomes overwhelming.

'Idris is very good with proportion – he brings space to all of my objects,' says Annie, referring to the brilliant and bizarre array of flea-market finds – everything from scraps of antique fabric to a collection of tiny dogs made from cockle shells – that weave throughout the house and set a fun, irreverent tone.

Walls in a colourful Matisse-esque paper by Christopher Farr enliven an otherwise dark upstairs hallway, along with one of Annie's drawings. At the end of the hall is the bathroom, with Charleston Farmhouse-inspired tiles and a vintage chair that Annie bought from Petworth Antiques Market.

'Annie finds things wherever she goes,' says Idris. 'Until I met her 17 years ago, I was heading towards a very minimal way of living, but she introduced me to a whole world of antique fabrics and patterns, and I now can't imagine living with white walls and clean lines,' he explains. 'I must bring a bit of restraint, though, because I'm sure she could have gone a lot crazier here.'

Take the little model of a man with a ball and chain attached to his leg: 'I found him at a flea market in France, wrapped him up in a fancy Tiffany box and gave him to Idris as a joke,' Annie recalls. Now he sits in the dining room, atop his own little plinth, next to one of Annie's stack sculptures and in front of an Art Deco mirror that the couple found in Petworth. 'I love that combination of junky bits with something really nice,' explains Annie, who has an encyclopedic knowledge of interiors and is visibly animated by her finds. 'Look at these pencils I bought from a house clearance in France,' she says, excitedly showing me bundles of pencils that have been grouped together by colour. 'I love how someone took the time to arrange them this way; they're basically their own art piece,' she muses.

Colour, more than perhaps anything else, is what draws Annie to things and it's her bold jewel-like palette that the interior is built on. 'I find colour hugely uplifting; it has the power to completely change my emotions,' she admits. Gavin helped them knit the interiors together, guiding on fabrics, paints and wallpapers to create a space that offers a zingy take on English country-house style. There are curtains and chairs in classic English patterns, but then there is also plenty that surprises, such as the upstairs corridor, which is papered — ceilings and all — in a colourful Christopher Farr design reminiscent of Matisse's cut-outs. 'The paper's a mad choice from Gavin, which gives such life to an otherwise bleak corridor,' says Idris. 'We've basically treated the tiniest space in the house like it's the grandest,' he adds, pointing out the green striped runner that marches up the stairs.

Green — a favourite colour of Gavin's (see his own house on pages 184–95) — plays out throughout the cottage, including in Annie and Idris's bedroom, which is papered top-to-toe in a diamond-and-foliage-adorned pattern (also in Gavin's own bedroom). This room is typical of the couple's approach to decorating: 'Pulling together interiors is a bit like creating a piece of art,' Annie reasons. 'Everything is a discussion and it's all about getting the balance right.' Here it happened to be a case of more is more: the bold wallpaper is matched by yet more patterns, introduced through a floral headboard and curtains, which are trimmed with an antique braid. A Donald Duck cushion, embroidered by Annie's mother, gives a playful pop, but it was only when the couple found an antique floral sheet for the bed — trimmed with a red-and-white striped scallop — that the room actually clicked. 'That and the old red-and-white stripe fabric that I've draped over the chair just tie the whole room together,' Annie explains. 'It's like a sculpture: you change one element and the whole piece changes.'

In another example of their unexpected approach to balance, the obviously grander, main spaces have been gently toned down. In the dining room, with its lofty proportions and pitched roof, the walls are the colour of a brown paper bag, while in the sitting room — the room in the house perhaps most grounded in English country-house style — soft white paint provides a foil for swathes of pretty curtains and deep sofas. 'We thought about going brighter with the paint, but the white actually makes all the other colours in here pop,' observes Annie. Here the crystallising piece was a mid-century red ceramic sculpture of a man. 'I found him at a market in France near where we have a house and that small dash of red just somehow makes sense of everything else in the room,' says Annie. Indeed, he joins the dots, picking up the reds of the rug on the floor, and giving energy to the traditional upholstery, including a sculptural leather sofa that belonged to Robert Kime, which the couple bought from his shop some years ago. Just as transformative for this room, though, was the little red, white and black mechanical horse sculpture that now sits on a side table on top of a Picasso book of the exact same colouring. 'I love his bold graphics and strong colours,' says Annie. 'Now they have found each other, they need to stay together,' she explains.

Just like in their art, the couple love to play with scale in rooms. In the kitchen, that comes from a huge splatter-style blue antique cupboard, which takes up an entire wall and sets the palette for the room. 'That piece sums up my approach to decorating,' says Idris. 'I like big pieces where it's basically maximum impact for minimal input.' It's the same with how the couple often display art too: 'We love putting big artworks in small spaces,' continues Idris, pointing out the painting in the entrance hall, by a contemporary artist friend of Annie's, which stretches across an entire wall. 'The colours in that are just so good,' adds Annie, who has complemented the lilac in the painting with a faded striped fabric, draped over the central table, which she found in Istanbul. 'It came from the same man that we bought the rug in the sitting room, and it wasn't really for sale, but we persuaded him,' she says, with a grin.

As in a work of art, this is an interior that deftly balances colour, shape and scale. But it is also ever-evolving, and the addition of Annie's next flea-market find could well give it an entirely new energy. And, of course, that is all part of the fun.

A small boot room space, painted in an olive
green, leads onto an entrance hall. A vast painting
by a contemporary artist friend of Annie's fills one
wall, while a central table is draped with a faded striped
fabric from Istanbul, which was in fact being used as
a curtain in a shop out there. Above the fireplace hangs
a Tracey Emin that the couple bought at a charity auction.

Designer Gavin Houghton suggested blue
for the kitchen walls and units, picking
up the colour of a huge splatter-style blue
antique cupboard that originally came from
a cottage in Cornwall. An ever-changing
display of drawings by the couple's
children hang behind the kitchen table.

BASELITZ-ACADEMY

The sitting room and dining room flow into each other. White walls in the former provide a backdrop to a sculptural leather sofa that once belonged to Robert Kime and a red figure of a man, which the couple bought from a market in France. The walls of the dining room are the colour of a brown paper bag, which provides an antidote to an Art Deco mirror and one of Annie's colourful 'Stack' sculptures.

1 CLOWN

The walls and ceiling of Annie and Idris's
bedroom are papered in the same Bloomsbury-
esque pattern that Gavin's bedroom (p.192)
is in. The clown poster came from the
Yves Saint Laurent Museum in Marrakech.
The starting point for the bathroom was the
Water Monopoly bath with its yellow ball
feet; the towels came from Annie's mother.

In the bathroom, chintz blinds contrast a zingy green tub. A curious collection of dogs, made from cockle shells and bought from a flea market, sit on the windowsill. Annie and Idris's son's bedroom reflects their love of stripes, while the rug and American folk art quilts are from a shop in Montecito that the couple often visit. The Conran Shop's 'Drew the Pencil Lamp' adds a playful edge.

GEORGE SAUMAREZ SMITH

Architect, Hampshire

For a house with trailing floral wallpapers, lively blue walls and a kitchen that deftly balances red, orange and blue, it is surprising to hear that its owner, architect George Saumarez Smith, took a while to embrace colour and pattern. 'They weren't part of my training at all,' explains George, a director at leading classical architecture practice Adam Architecture, who lives in Winchester. 'What I do is all about line, tone and proportion, and with drawings, it's all monochrome.' He does, however, recall growing up amongst the wallpapers that his grandparents – his grandfather, Raymond Erith, was also a renowned classical architect – and parents had chosen to deck their houses out in. 'William Morris was a staple, but I always slightly associated his patterns with uncomfortable sofas and faded fabrics,' he admits.

His eureka moment came about 10 years ago, when he started slowly collecting furniture, pictures and rugs. 'It felt like the more I put in, the more the house began to feel like it was working how it was intended to,' he explains. Built in the 1860s, it is a classic semi-detached villa, with lowerground, raised ground and first floors, and a long garden that backs onto more of the same. When George bought it in the early 2000s, beige and greige were in their heyday, and he decorated in an accordingly sparse style. After a few years, he started to buy old brown furniture from local auctions – out of practicality rather than any kind of aesthetic rebellion. 'It was a cheap way to fill empty spaces and make better use of the house,' he recalls. 'I realised, however, that there was something very comforting about these old beaten-up pieces,' he says, pointing out a sideboard in the dining room that he bought for £20 at auction. Soon, the pieces began to increase in calibre, as George developed a love for the elegance of late Regency furniture, especially Gillows.

With brown added to the palette, the house soon became rather more colourful when George started collecting linocuts by printmaker Sheila Robinson, who was one of the Great Bardfield set's lesser-known artists, alongside the likes of Edward Bawden and Eric Ravilious. George started buying one or two of her prints, but quickly ended up buying a dozen in one go after meeting Robinson's daughter, Chloë Cheese. Now he has over 30. 'That's how I decorate, I guess,' George explains. 'There will be a rush of activity and then the interiors generally go back to a fairly stable state for a while.' But the addition of Robinson's prints – rich with oranges, muddy blues and greens – in fact prompted another spate of activity. 'She uses colour in such interesting ways and I decided they couldn't just hang on grey walls,' George explains. Around the same time, he was regularly visiting India for a project he was working on, and he would return from each trip with block-printed fabrics, which soon started to find their way onto beds and tables at home.

George Saumarez Smith's dining room is papered in 'Indian' by Morris & Co, and the cat print is one of many in the house by printmaker Sheila Robinson, whose work George has collected for over 20 years. The dining room connects to the kitchen.

And so it was that his house started to really embrace colour and pattern, tempered by his architect's eye and a commitment to doing what felt right for the house. Inspired by his stash of Robinson's prints, the first paper he chose was one of hers – 'Monkeys and Birds', now produced by St Jude's – which provides a joyful backdrop to the lower-ground garden-facing spare bedroom. In the raised ground-floor dining room, he opted for 'Indian' by Morris & Co, a gold and black indienne-inspired floral design – not by William Morris, but the architect George Gilbert Scott – which dates back to 1868. 'I chose this because it reminded me of all of the Indian textiles I'd fallen in love with on trips out there,' he explains. The fact it is a contemporary with the house is also not lost on George. 'I'm not a purist, but I am drawn to things that match the house's age.' He also used the pattern in the red and blue colourway, as a backdrop to the beautiful bookshelves he designed for the lower-ground library. 'I basically designed the bookshelves to fit as many books as possible and even now I'm running out of space,' he explains. George's father was a bookseller and George, judging by the shelves crammed full of interesting tomes, also caught the bug. 'Books are a bad habit of mine, but they definitely make this house what it is.' He admits that he is still making his mind up on the wallpaper down here. 'Sometimes you only really see what works by trying things out and I may well change this one, but the logistics are a bit complicated due to all the book-moving involved.'

George is fine with making mistakes and sees them as a vital part of the decorating process. The kitchen, for instance, is a space that has worn many guises before it reached today's combination of colours, which enliven the stainless-steel Bulthaup island that has sat in the centre of the space since soon after George bought the house. In fact, the decision to add colour came about through a bit of a mishap when the lower ground floor flooded, causing George to drape a couple of Persian rugs from down there over the Aga to dry out. 'I realised how much their colours made a difference to the space, which back then was all grey,' he explains. The colours in the rug found their way into the room – a custard yellow for the walls, red for one run of cupboards and a bluey-green for the other. But something did not feel right: 'It felt like traffic lights,' admits George, laughing. He had a rethink and landed on today's incarnation, with walls in Edward Bulmer's 'Dutch Orange', and cupboards in 'Porphyry Red' and 'Spa Blue' – both by Papers and Paints. They are strong tones, but feel completely perfect together.

The hallway, filled with prints, architectural drawings and plaster mouldings, is equally punchy in colour, painted in Farrow & Ball's 'Stone Blue'. 'I would never have chosen this strong a colour when I moved in, and I probably wouldn't have chosen it five years ago either, but the house can take it,' George says. It leads onto his study – a small but captivating space, just a little wider than a sash window, which is painted in 'Inchyra Blue', a bluey-green by Farrow & Ball. 'I love blues and greens, but I found that slightly greener blues were better at the back, which is north-facing, while brighter blues worked better for the south-facing side,' he explains. The hallway and staircase also provide a transition from what George describes as the 'more traditional' downstairs to the slightly fresher upstairs. 'I like the way that Sir John Soane's house in Lincoln's Inn Fields feels very archaeological and heavy downstairs, and is then much lighter upstairs, with that yellow drawing room on the first floor,' George says. 'Of course, I'm not at all comparing my little house to that, but I like that idea of layers and different stories within one space.'

In many ways, this is an apt comparison, for this is a house that has evolved layer by layer and ultimately represents a love of collecting that has created a warm and uplifting interior. It is slow decorating at its very best.

A stainless steel Bulthaup kitchen island sits in
pleasing contrast to traditional joinery painted
in 'Spa Blue' by Papers and Paints and walls
in Edward Bulmer's 'Dutch Orange'. A shelf of
beloved English Mochaware sits above the Aga.
The hallway, lined with architectural drawings and
prints, is painted in 'Stone Blue' by Farrow & Ball.

George's study, just off the ground floor hallway, packs a punch, painted in 'Inchyra Blue' by Farrow & Ball and hung with architectural drawings. The cosy basement library is papered in 'Indian' by Morris & Co in the red and blue colourway; the bookshelves were designed bespoke by George to fit as many books as possible in.

The basement guest bedroom is
papered in Sheila Robinson's 'Monkeys
and Birds', which is available from St
Jude's; the ensuite bathroom is painted
in Farrow & Ball's 'Sugar Bag Light',
with acid green tiles from Emery et Cie.

TESS & ALFRED NEWALL

Decorative artist; and furniture designer and maker, East Sussex

Jill Barklem's iconic *Brambly Hedge* books, chronicling and illustrating the adventures of a community of mice living in charmingly decorated tree trunks and hedgerows, are a firm favourite in the Newall household. Perhaps it is not coincidental, then, that Tess and Alfred Newall's mid-sixteenth-century timber-framed house in East Sussex, which they share with their three young children, feels like it could have sprung from the pages depicting this enchanting world. Sitting at the foot of the South Downs, just off the coach road that leads to Charleston Farmhouse, it is all oak beams, (painted) flowers climbing the walls, hops hanging from the ceiling, canopied beds and pretty floral fabrics. Tess and Alfred may not be whipping up primrose puddings or combing the hedgerows for supplies, but they are just as industrious – Alfred designs and makes beautiful wooden furniture, and is pretty much single-handedly responsible for reviving the bobbin leg, while Tess is a hugely successful decorative artist, who turns her exquisite hand to everything from circus-tent-inspired whole-room murals to children's chairs.

This is a house where the handcrafted matters: much of the interior has been made by them, from walls papered in a magical wild floral design that Tess created especially for their girls' room, to the bobbin beds that Alfred made for each of their children. 'I love that they sleep in beds that I built for

them,' he says. 'It feels really rewarding to make things for our house,' adds the furniture maker, who also designed and made the oak and Douglas fir kitchen, where a large and very *Brambly Hedge*-appropriate built-in dresser and plate rack take centre stage. 'We didn't have cupboards for a year, as our house always comes last,' says Tess, with a laugh. 'But it means so much that Alfred built our kitchen,' she adds. 'There's a real satisfaction when things operate well, and there's extra pleasure when it's something you've thought about and made yourself,' Alfred agrees.

The couple bought the house in 2019. They had been living in a small studio flat in west London, but with their now oldest son on the cusp of walking and a frustrating lack of nearby studio space (Tess was renting somewhere in Hackney and Alfred was driving a couple of hours each day to a studio in Essex), they decided it was time for a change. 'There wasn't an obvious place in the countryside, but we didn't want to be too far from London, as that's where a lot of our work is,' explains Tess. 'I had this vision of a Thomas Hardy farmhouse with workshops attached, but we quickly realised our budget wasn't going to stretch to that.' A friend's mum, who knew they were on a house-hunt, emailed them a link to this house, which until the 1950s was two – one dating to the mid-sixteenth century and one to the mid-seventeenth-century. 'We saw it at

This part of the kitchen occupies the extension, with the doors, inspired by the coppery falu red often used for the exterior of rural Swedish houses, painted in Little Greene's 'Baked Cherry'. The antique Orkney chair was bought at auction in Edinburgh.

its worst on a miserable winter day, but we immediately knew it was the one,' explains Tess. The surrounding landscape, with the Downs majestically rising up from the bottom of the garden, was a big part of its appeal, but so too was the fact it was timber-framed. 'I looked at it almost as if it was a piece of furniture,' Alfred recalls. 'It's amazing how oak just gets stronger and stronger,' he adds.

And so they moved in, living in it for a year while they dreamed up their plans for the space. It is largely one-room deep, with a kitchen, sitting room and bathroom on the ground floor, and the bedrooms upstairs. While the bones were good, it had been subject to a fair few alterations over the years. 'Our aim was to take it back to how it should have been,' says Tess. Visits to the Weald and Downland Living Museum near Chichester – an amazing open-air museum with 50 or so rescued historic buildings – gave them an insight into the details that might be lurking under false ceilings, and they called on Rabble Architecture, a local studio headed up by Will Anderson, to help them return the space to its former glory, restoring the timbers and extending the kitchen to create a space that would stand up to the demands of family life. They moved to a small cottage down the road and the year-long renovations began. In the kitchen, a 1970s ceiling was pulled down to reveal a beautiful timber-framed smoke bay – one of the earliest types of chimneys. 'It was a leap of faith, but Will thought the beams would be lurking and, thankfully, they were,' says Alfred. Fake ceilings were also removed upstairs, turning what would become the two children's bedrooms into the stuff of fairytales.

Rather like the murals that Tess creates for clients, the house's palette is softly colourful. There are exposed plaster walls, burnt oranges, blues, pinks, reds and browns – all colours that have a bearing in some way on the natural world. Tess mainly chose colours and paints, Alfred led on joinery, and fabric decisions were a joint endeavour. 'We didn't really lay out schemes, but just let rooms evolve,' explains Tess. 'I like colour, but muddy versions of it.' The doors that flank the kitchen extension are a good example, painted in what Tess describes as an 'old-fashioned' red. 'They're partly inspired by falu red, which is the coppery colour often used for the exterior of rural Swedish houses,' explains Tess, who regularly looks to the Scandinavian country for decorative inspiration for her work and often adds burnt umber – a brown – to tone down the intensity of colours in her murals. While the kitchen doors provide a pop of colour, they also feel entirely in keeping with the limewash walls, Orkney chair, wicker pendant, beautiful early nineteenth-century hand-painted Austrian cabinet and under-cupboard curtains made from a screenprinted floral from Nicholas Herbert.

Next door, in the sitting room, Edward Bulmer's 'Brick' provides a backdrop, applied in a wash to the ceilings and walls. 'It's a low-ceilinged room, and we wanted to make it feel warm and slightly Mediterranean,' explains Tess. 'It was a bit of a job applying it to our walls, as they're so rough, but it was all about working with the house,' she adds. For the original inglenook fireplace, the couple opted for hand-painted blue and white Delft-style tiles from Douglas Watson. 'It's our version of a *kakelugn*,' says Tess, referring to traditional Swedish tiled stoves. A sofa upholstered in a stripe from Robert Kime creates a division between the sitting area and the children's play area, where a wall of bobbin shelves, made by Alfred, provides ample storage for toys. 'Both of us never want our work to be too precious and are big believers that things only get nicer when they're used,' Alfred explains. 'Although I'm hoping the girls won't draw on the wallpaper in their bedroom,' says Tess, with a smile. 'They're quite keen on doodling on the walls in the sitting room, but it's just paint in there, so it isn't the end of the world.'

Upstairs is more theatrical. For starters, there is something resembling a circus tent on the landing, with navy tongue-and-groove walls and majestic red-and-white fabric top. In fact, the little cubicle cleverly conceals a loo and washbasin, while a bath sits on the other side of the room, under the window. 'It was the only way we could squeeze a family bathroom into the upstairs, and the children love it,' says Tess, who rigged the fabric up using a frame that she sourced from a curtain maker. The girls' bedroom is particularly playful, with the wildflowers of Tess's own 'Secret Garden' wallpaper climbing up the walls and onto the newly exposed original beamed ceiling. A pair of Alfred's bobbin beds have been transformed into the sort you would find in *Brambly Hedge*, with half-canopies magicked up from raspberry and rose checks. 'I guess I wanted to create for the girls the sort of princess beds that I always dreamed of when I was a child,' says Tess, who had frilly Liberty print lampshades made to go by each bed. 'I love how the canopies make the most of the height of the room, but also create the feeling of a den.'

Like many others in this book, Tess and Alfred don't necessarily see their home as ever being finished. In part, this is because both struggle to let their own house become a job on their books, but also because they have always approached it as an ever-evolving space. And although their workshops are a few miles down the road, their house in many ways is an extension of their studios – a testing ground and a place to enjoy their creations. 'We'd like to decorate the house a bit more, but it takes time because we'd rather hold off and wait to use our own designs,' Tess explains. No doubt, it will be well worth the wait.

Tess and Alfred's earthy, softly colourful palette comes together beautifully in the kitchen, with an early nineteenth-century hand-painted Austrian cabinet, an under-cupboard curtain made from Nicholas Herbert's 'Coromandel' design and a small bobbin shelf unit on the wall, which, along with the kitchen, was made by Alfred.

Edward Bulmer's 'Brick', applied as a wash, provides a warm backdrop to the sitting room and playroom. The ottoman is covered in an antique suzani, while the sofa is upholstered in 'Tynemouth Ticking' from Robert Kime. Behind it are a couple of ceramic Italian table lamps, bought from the hilltop town of Gubbio and topped with fabric lampshades by Alice Palmer.

Beware
of the bull

Upstairs, the two childrens rooms are
connected. Both feature Alfred's bobbin
beds, with the pair in the further room
decked out in half-canopies made from
Salvesen Graham's 'Little Check' fabric
in the raspberry and rose colourways.
The walls and ceilings in this room are lined
with Tess's own 'Secret Garden' wallpaper.

The upstairs landing plays host to a family
bathroom, with the loo and sink contained
within a theatrical circus tent whipped up from
tongue-and-groove (painted in a lightened
version of Farrow & Ball's 'Hague Blue') and
a striped Ian Mankin fabric top. The blind is
made from Namay Samay's 'Noor' in mughal.

LUCINDA CHAMBERS

Stylist and designer, west London

'I find the process of styling a room is very similar to decorating a body,' says Lucinda Chambers, the legendary fashion stylist known for her playful approach to colour, print and texture. 'It's all about putting colours together that have some sort of conversation and provoke a reaction,' she explains. 'I think clothes and interiors should both be about creating the most joyous experience.'

Joyous, certainly, is the word that springs to mind at Lucinda's house in Shepherd's Bush, where a kaleidoscope of colour unfolds behind an otherwise ordinary Victorian facade. There are walls crammed full of ceramics and art, and cheerful yellow and red rooms so resplendent that they cannot help but raise spirits. 'I see every surface as a colour opportunity, whether it's a skirting board, the inside of a cupboard or a ceiling,' says Lucinda. 'I get restless and I'd honestly paint the back of the door if I hadn't got anything else to do.' She, of course, has plenty to do – she spent 25 years as the fashion director at *British Vogue*, until 2017, before co-founding fashion brand Colville and e-commerce platform Collagerie – but this says a lot about her hands-on approach to decorating. She is a woman of projects – everything from painting to making a mosaic table out of ceramic casualties – and her house, which has evolved slowly but hugely over 30 years, is testament to that.

Lucinda and her husband, Simon Crow, bought the Victorian terrace in the early 1990s and have raised their three boys there. Other than tripling the size of the kitchen to create a charming space that runs the width of the house, they kept the bones as they were. There is a kitchen, dining room and sitting room on the ground floor; the drawing room and main bedroom are on the first floor, and four additional bedrooms on the upper two floors. 'I'm actually quite afraid of spatial transformation,' admits Lucinda, who, by an ironic twist, grew up watching her mother pull down the walls of the houses they lived in. 'We'd moved 18 times before I was 17,' Lucinda recalls. 'She'd buy these poky old houses and start knocking the walls down to create totally different spaces. She was brilliant at it.'

On the contrary, the changes at Lucinda's house have been wrought through paint and what she modestly refers to as 'layers of love and clutter'. Some rooms, such as the electric-yellow dining room and the Pompeiian-red drawing room, have been the same colour for 20 or so years. 'I don't redecorate for the sake of it, but always when things are getting beyond shabby.' Similarly, she never uses colour for colour's sake: 'I spend a lot of time thinking about how we'll use the room and whether the colour needs to be soft and calm or lively and energising.' Sometimes it is completely enveloping, such as in the television sitting-room, where Lucinda painted the walls in a warm red

The walls of Lucinda's television sitting room are painted in Little Greene's 'Firefly', with a playful strip of 'Mister David' above the picture rail. Rugs, including the 'Super Shaggy' rug from Lucinda's own brand Colville, are layered up on the floor, while 12 Oka prints hang on the wall.

to amp up the space's cosy appeal. 'It almost feels like it's on fire,' she enthuses. 'It used to be our boys' playroom, but since we've claimed it back, it's become a bit of a TV supper den for us.'

While the house hangs together brilliantly, Lucinda confesses that she rarely thinks about the colour relationships between the rooms. 'I don't give much thought to how one room leads to the next, but there are threads of colour that hold it all together,' she explains. 'It's a bit like when I'm dressing and I might wear green eyeliner to pick up the green of my socks.' Reds crop up not just on walls, but also in the candy-cane stripe of the dining-room sofa, the punchy red Aga in the kitchen (a fortuitous relic from the previous owners) and the rugs layered on the drawing-room floor. Yellow is another colour that weaves throughout the house, not just on the dining-room walls, but as a border above the picture rail in the television sitting-room and on the bathtub in Lucinda's bathroom. 'I painted that 30 years ago,' she says of the bath, which sits beneath a wall, painted in a shade of gardener's twine. 'I actually painted this room turquoise once and it was just so horribly unrestful that I ended up painting it back the next day,' she says. 'I've made a lot of colour fails over the years, but that is how you work out what is right.'

While the world of fashion is one of trends, Lucinda is not a fervent follower. 'There are trends I watch with interest, but I'm much more interested in working out my own relationship with style and getting my inspiration from nature or exhibitions,' she explains. 'It was the same when I was at *Vogue*. I'd never really look at the catwalk and was much more interested in creating my own narrative for a story.' Like the shoots she's masterminded, she is particularly good at introducing discordant elements into an interior. 'I can't bear anything too blended,' she explains. A case in point is one of her spare bedrooms – a recent project that she has been painting in snatched hours over a few weeks – where she has replaced the graffitied walls from her son's days with a palette of chiffon

greys and blues for the walls, and tobacco for the ceiling, which she colour-matched to a candle. 'It was all getting a bit ghastly good taste and I decided it needed a modern orange chair to knock things off,' she says. 'I was explaining my dilemma to some friends we were visiting one weekend and they happened to have this electric-orange chair in their attic that they were trying to get rid of. It's bonkers, but perfect.'

As much as the house is shaped by colour, it is also defined by the collections it plays host to. Many of these have also arisen from an urge to venture out of her comfort zone. 'I started collecting studio pottery about 10 years ago because I found it quite ugly and challenging, but I've grown to love it,' she says. 'I like it when something sharpens the mind.' Ceramics more broadly play a huge part in Lucinda's life and there is not a room where a vase or plate does not adorn a surface, including in her bathroom, with its wall of colourful plates. For many years, the dining room has been less a place for eating and more a holding pen for ceramics, before they find their way to a surface elsewhere – and she has recently made use of a blank wall in the kitchen by having a dresser of turquoise shelves built in to hold yet more ceramics. 'I had to find a way to get them off the kitchen floor and onto the wall,' she says, grinning. 'I'm a total magpie, and my strength and weakness is that I see the point of many things,' says Lucinda, who spends weekends and holidays rummaging through car boot sales and markets. 'I love pushing myself and buying things that I don't necessarily see in my house,' she says, citing a 1970s poster that she recently bought as an example. A gatherer she may be, but she is not at all precious about having a clear-out when the house starts reaching a tipping point. 'I can recognise when I need to have a declutter.'

For a house that feels so relevant to today, it is remarkable that many parts have been that way for a couple of decades or more. Equally, it is a house where parts, no matter how small they may be, are always changing. Pieces come and go, and layers evolve – and that, of course, is integral to its charm.

The kitchen is relatively neutral in its palette, save for the white and brown checkered lino floor and pop of red that comes in from the Aga, which Lucinda inherited when she bought the house. The plate rack, painted in 'Light Blue' by Farrow & Ball, was added to accommodate Lucinda's growing collection of ceramics, occupying an otherwise blank wall.

Lucinda painted the dining room electric yellow over 20 years ago – it is Papers and Paints' bespoke PP27-8-21JG – while the upstairs drawing room is painted in a warm Pompeiian red with Moroccan and Turkish rugs underfoot.

Lucinda's bedroom is serene, painted in a bespoke colour
that Lucinda had mixed 25 years ago. Her husband, Simon Crow,
drew the design for the woodwork around the fireplace on the back
of an envelope, while a friend of Lucinda's added the mosaic mirrors
around it. The wardrobes are lined with different floral fabrics,
bought from vintage textile fairs in London and France. In Lucinda's
ensuite, the colour comes not from the walls – painted in Farrow &
Ball's 'String' – but from the yellow bathtub and colourful array of
plates hung on the wall. Collected from flea markets and car boot
sales and never costing more than £10 each, they take centre stage.

LUKE EDWARD HALL & DUNCAN CAMPBELL

Designer and artist; and artist, Gloucestershire

I first met Luke Edward Hall and Duncan Campbell in 2014, when Luke was working in the interiors team for architectural designer Ben Pentreath. As a side hustle, he was selling some rather lovely cushions embroidered with Ionic columns and octopus motifs, while Duncan had just co-founded creative consultancy Campbell-Rey with Charlotte Rey. Skip forward 10 years, and Luke and Duncan, now husbands, are something of a *tour de force* in the design world, sitting at the centre of an eclectic style that embraces colour, pattern and whimsy. Luke is an artist, designer and *Financial Times* interiors columnist – with a hotel, fashion brand, and many a drawing and collaboration under his belt – while Duncan, still at the helm of Campbell-Rey, has broadened the studio's remit to everything from huge interiors projects to furniture and glassware collections.

For years, the couple had called a playfully decorated one-bedroom flat in Camden home, but in 2019 they got the urge to rent somewhere in a rather more rural setting. While they dreamed of castellated gatehouses and follies ('Basically, anything the Landmark Trust would have,' quips Duncan, referring to the holiday-rental company that specialises in historic buildings), they eventually committed to a three-bedroom cottage down a secluded lane on the edge of an estate in Gloucestershire. 'It's a very ordinary shepherd's cottage, which has nothing around it other than amazing views in every direction,' explains Duncan of the house. 'When we first visited, it was a very grey day in March, but we loved the fact that it feels airy downstairs rather than like a warren of tiny rooms,' Luke adds, referring to the ground floor layout, which consists of an open-plan sitting area and kitchen, and separate dining room.

For two people who make a living from transforming spaces, it is perhaps surprising that they were so thrilled at the prospect of a rental where there was limited scope for change. 'The kitchen and bathrooms were in good nick, so all we had to do was paint the walls, which was perfect,' says Luke, explaining that the couple, who have lived there most of the time since lockdown, initially intended to use it as a weekend retreat. In many ways, they approached it as an antidote to their work lives: 'We never wanted this place to be about interior design schemes and just thought, let's fill it with friends and dogs and a big chintzy sofa,' says Duncan. 'Although we both love our own projects, we didn't want this to feel like a job, and it felt massively liberating that we didn't have to produce concept boards for every decision we made,' he adds.

To begin with, they camped out and bought a few bits and bobs from local junk shops and auctions to fill obvious gaps – a big old farmhouse table for long weekend lunches, beds for

the spare bedrooms and shelves to house their ever-growing collection of books. 'We basically indulged in everything that our little London flat couldn't offer us,' says Duncan. 'I wanted little jewel-box rooms stuffed with things,' says Luke, who admits to being an inveterate collector of everything, from prints and drawings to chairs. Their approach to decorating here, they suggest, was bolder than it might have been, partly because they never saw it as their full-time home. 'It's not totally frivolous, but I guess we thought it was somewhere we'd come at weekends and be in a more relaxed frame of mind,' says Duncan. 'We wanted our friends to come here and immediately feel relaxed, which has really shaped how we decorated. I guess it was all about conviviality.'

The couple started by picking paint colours or wallpapers for each room, many of which have since changed, following a fire at the cottage in January 2023. Thankfully, it caused little more damage than smoking everything out, but it did provide the chance for a bit of a palette change. 'I actually think we picked the colours too quickly the first time round, so once we'd got over the hideousness of the fire admin, it was actually quite a good opportunity,' says Duncan. The mustard yellow in the dining room was replaced by Edward Bulmer's warm 'Red Ochre', while one of the guest rooms went from a zingy blue to Little Greene's cocooning 'Light Bronze Green'. Downstairs, the living area was painted in Edward Bulmer's restful 'Nicaragua', while the kitchen cupboards were given a lick of mustard yellow – Little Greene's 'Tan'.

The entire house is something of a testing ground. In the bedroom, desperate to try out an over-the-top floral wallpaper, they opted for a jazzy design from Christopher Moore, while in the sitting room, Luke commissioned an ottoman and had the top embroidered with golden arrows. 'Lots of the house was about scratching an itch and trying things we'd always wanted to,' says Duncan. The headboards in the bedrooms were another playful experiment, designed by the couple to resemble a pagoda and pediment. Do they ever disagree? 'Very rarely,' says Duncan. 'We love so many of the same things,' says Luke, reeling off a list of examples that range from *trompe l'oeil* and papier mâché, as well as rococo and baroque-inspired pieces. 'Anything shaped like a shell, painted Regency or faintly ridiculous gets our attention,' Duncan adds.

While Luke and Duncan collect pieces independently from each other, they have found themselves bidding on the same pieces at auction. Recently, they nearly got into a sticky spot with the charming blue Dutch chest of drawers that now sits beautifully alongside the red walls of the dining room. 'I'd actually shown it to a client and then Luke sent a link over to me a few days later,' says Duncan. 'Thankfully, the client didn't want it!' Their approach is to buy the pieces they love, even if there is not an obvious spot for them. 'It happens a lot, and we'll find a piece of furniture calling to us,' Duncan explains. Equally, they stress that they try not to be too attached to what they buy and enjoy the fact it is all something of a moveable feast. 'The kind of interiors we like are those that develop over time,' explains Luke.

And so, while there was some quick whipping into shape when they moved in, the decoration of the house is a more leisurely affair, continually shifting and changing. 'You should never finish a house all at once,' Duncan says. 'This cottage for us isn't about acquiring things, but about making the small things in life a joy.' Ultimately, it's a place where fun, comfort and joy reign supreme.

The walls of the dining room are painted in
Edward Bulmer's 'Red Ochre', which provides
a backdrop to a Campbell Rey for Nordic Knots
rug and a set of Vico Magistretti dining chairs,
made by Cassina and sold through Habitat
in the 1960s. The blue Dutch chest of drawers
came from antiques dealer Adam Bentley.

The bathroom, painted in Farrow & Ball's
'Arsenic' is a nod to the one at Charleston
Farmhouse in Sussex. The romantic
1980s-esque blind was made from pink silk
leftover from a project, while the shelves play
host to beautifully packaged soaps from the
likes of Santa Maria Novella and Officine Buly.

The guest bedroom is painted in
Little Greene's 'Light Bronze Green',
while Luke and Duncan's bedroom is
resplendent in Christopher Moore's
'Rosemaine'. Both rooms feature a
headboard designed by the couple
to resemble a pagoda and a pediment.

HOLLY HOWE

Designer, north London

O f all the houses in this book, this has to be the one that I feel most connected to. Not least because its owner, Holly Howe, is a friend, but also because I lived in the flat opposite for a year and witnessed the sweat and tears that went into transforming this Victorian end-of-terrace into the colourful and imaginative home that Holly, her husband Alexis and two young boys call home today. There were weekends of pulling up dusty carpets and ripping out clunky built-in furniture, and every few weeks or so they would pack up and move to a different floor to make way for the builders. Alongside all of this, Holly was hard at work, overseeing the builders, picking paint colours and sourcing everything, from vintage lighting to replacement floorboard nails and screws, which she patinated herself to make sure they felt right for the house's Victorian bones. 'No detail escaped me,' she says, grinning. 'It's in my genes.'

Holly is the co-creative director of Howe, the antiques shop founded over 35 years ago by her father, the renowned dealer and designer Christopher Howe. Today, the Pimlico Road stalwart is known not just for its astonishing inventory of antiques, but also for its impeccably crafted collection of furniture and lighting. Holly is at the helm of the recently launched Howe Home collection — an edit of ready-to-go staples, inspired by Howe's antiques and existing designs,

as well as pieces Holly has developed for her own home. Holly and Alexis bought this house between lockdowns in September 2020, attracted to the fact it is on a leafy street, just a skip from Hampstead Heath, and had not been fiddled about with. 'Even though most of the windows had been blacked out or curtains taped shut, we could tell that there was this amazing light and atmosphere,' says Holly of the property, which is spread across three floors, plus an attic. 'It felt a bit like Mary Poppins' handbag,' she adds, explaining that while the house's end-of-terrace spot meant they had some wonky angles to contend with, they also gained an extra wedge of space at the back.

First up, it was a matter of getting the structure right. The roof was replaced and the flank wall was tied in. Then it was a case of maximising the layout: the kitchen moved from a poky room at the back to the main living space, which runs the depth of the house; the attic was opened up to create an extra bedroom; and an ensuite was created for the main bedroom on the third floor. 'We had a very white house before and we really wanted to use more colour here,' explains Holly, who previously lived in a small mews house on the other side of the Heath. 'The fact we had more rooms to play with than in our old house made me feel like we could have a lot more fun in the decoration.' Even so, she is not the sort to put

Raw plaster walls provide a calming backdrop to Holly Howe's main living area. The buttermilk joinery around the fireplace was designed by Holly's father, the antiques dealer Christopher Howe, while the armchair is Made by Howe's 'Retriever', upholstered in 'Squiggle' from Howe at 36 Bourne Street. The green table is Howe's 'Bombay Button Table'.

a scheme or moodboard together. 'I instinctively felt what the colours should be for each room and got straight to painting a patchwork of green samples on the wall to pick the perfect uplifting green for the study-office,' says Holly, referring to the first floor room that had previously been used as the main bedroom.

Green is a colour that features throughout the house. 'I think it might be because we live in such a green area that the colour just found its way indoors,' Holly suggests. Downstairs, she has paired the waxed plaster walls of the open-plan kitchen, dining and living space with dark green floorboards and curtains made from vintage linen sheets, hand-dyed by her Howe colleague James Townend in a grassy green colour. 'He's an incredible colour alchemist,' says Holly. The sitting area is cosy, confined to the back of the room, with a small Howe corner sofa and a couple of armchairs opposite, which can be easily moved, depending on which side of the room is being used. 'I always say that blue is my favourite colour, but I am starting to think I might be wrong about that,' says Holly, gesturing to a wooden fairground banner emblazoned with the word 'Superb' and a 1960s Swedish tapestry rug, which both feature leafy greens. That said, her old favourite is also weaved throughout, in upholstered pieces, fabrics and, in the case of her son's bedroom – which is painted in glossy dark-blue linseed paint from Brouns & Co – on the walls. The colour is most resplendent in what they now tellingly refer to as the childrens' 'blue bathroom', which is wrapped in sky-blue, with tongue-and-groove panelling and a 1950s bathroom suite. 'I found the bath and sink for a steal on Facebook Marketplace,' explains Holly, who used Broken Bog – a company that specialises in colourful vintage sanitaryware – to find a loo in the same shade.

'I liked the idea of rooms being identifiable by their colour,' she explains. Another case in point is their ensuite bathroom, which is a pretty confection of pale pink tiles and a pink sink that had been sitting around in Howe's warehouse for a decade or more, owing to the fact it had a huge crack in it. 'We found this amazing specialist called The Bath Business who repaired the crack,' Holly adds. The guest bathroom is rather punchier, with yellow and white stripes, and chequerboard tiles in the same colours. 'It was inspired by a bathroom that I remember from childhood holidays in the countryside,' recalls Holly. Finding the right tiles in lockdown became something of an endurance

event, and Holly spent evenings ordering samples and trying to find the right shade of yellow. Her bedroom is also a rather lovely yellow affair, papered in Howe's lively 'Pondicherry' floral design.

While most of the rooms are rich with colour and pattern, Holly made the decision to paint the hall and staircase white. 'It's a white spine that glues it all together,' says Holly. 'It's a bit like a palate cleanser between rooms.' Holly is particularly good at balancing the playful and calm – take, for instance, the buttermilk units in the kitchen, which were made by one of Howe's workshops in Norfolk and bring a softness to the space, especially with the worktop, made out of a single piece of oak that was meticulously planed into shape on site to fit the curved wall. Opposite the kitchen units, cupboards and joinery in the same delicious buttermilk were added around the existing fireplace. 'We owe this joinery to my dad, who drew it all up,' says Holly. 'He has such an amazing understanding of proportion and traditional construction, which really shows through the subtleties of the design.'

Unsurprisingly for a dealer's daughter, Holly has an excellent eye for antiques, which she has slowly collected from fairs and auctions. A handful of pieces came from the auction at Wormington Grange in 2021, including the pretty lantern in their sitting area and a stripey blue armchair that Holly upholstered in Howe fabric. Other pieces, including a set of original limewashed Heal's furniture in Holly's bedroom and the eighteenth century toleware flowers that adorn the kitchen fireplace, were also lucky auction finds. In Bertie's bedroom, the charming single four-poster bed is an antique Irish one that Howe sourced some time ago from favourite dealer friend John Evetts, which they are planning to use as the basis for a new design. 'My house has informed what I think people might want at Howe,' Holly explains.

Holly grew up watching the environment around her regularly change. In fact, at the age of five, she would pack her belongings into bags and take them with her wherever she went, in order to prevent them from disappearing and being replaced by something her parents thought was even better. This house, she admits, is not a space in quite that much flux, but she acknowledges that it will always evolve. 'I doubt the house will ever be complete, because that's the fun of it,' says Holly. 'Wouldn't it be awful if you went to an antiques fair and couldn't buy anything because you'd finished a space?'

Holly designed the kitchen and had it made by
a workshop in Norfolk. The oval kitchen table is
a vintage piece by William Tillman, while the kitchen
chairs are original 'BA3' chairs by twentieth century
designer Ernest Race. In the upstairs office, the
walls are painted in Edward Bulmer's 'Evie', with
a 1940s Turkish dhurrie underfoot and an armchair
that Holly bought at the Wormington Grange
auction in 2021 and had reupholstered.

In the family bathroom, the woodwork is painted in Little Greene's 'Grey Stone', while the walls are papered in Howe at 36 Bourne Street's 'Cypress Cocoa'. The 1950s bath and sink came from Facebook Marketplace, and a loo in the same shade was sourced separately from Broken Bog. The turtle print is a favourite find from a nearby antiques shop on Flask Walk in Hampstead.

Holly and her husband's bedroom is papered
in Howe at 36 Bourne Street's 'Pondicherry'
in the maize colourway, while the bedside table
is Howe Home's 'Le Bedside'. The tiles in the
bathroom were sourced from Walls and Floors.
Their son's playroom is two-tone: the top part
is painted in Edward Bulmer's 'Vert de Mer', while
the bottom half is a scrubbable bespoke off-white.

MAX HURD

Creative consultant, north-west London

I suspected that a whole lot of fun was about to unfold the moment I pressed Max Hurd's doorbell and was greeted by a trippy, high-pitched tune. 'It was a normal ding-dong when I first moved in, but we had to overhaul some of the electrics and we somehow ended up with this,' says Max, who bought the house in north-west London in 2021 after roughly six months of looking. 'The best thing about the doorbell is that it doesn't really stop, even when I open the door,' he says, laughing.

It sets the tone perfectly for this house, which also does not really stop, brimming with clashing colours, patterns and beloved trinkets. The hallway alone makes clear that this is not your typical Victorian terrace: a raucously patterned runner playfully parades up the stairs, while on your right a three and a half-metre long boldly coloured painting by Norton Saliba provides something of a surprise if you're expecting a row of coat hooks. Equally unexpected is the fact that Max bought the house almost entirely on the basis that it could accommodate this artwork. 'I would walk into houses with my measuring tape to see if it would fit, so as soon as I saw this corridor, I knew it was the one,' explains the creative consultant, who grew up with the painting at his childhood home in Brazil. 'It brings me so much joy.'

Joy, in fact, is the house's overriding theme. 'I wanted to create something that was fun and visually inspiring, but didn't take itself too seriously,' explains Max, whose background is in fashion and art direction. In a way, the house feels like a flamboyant set, with pink drapery suspended in the upstairs hallway and a theatrical shell-emblazoned headboard in Max's bedroom, sitting under yet more swathes of fabric. 'I think my mum thought I was a bit insane when I described my ideas for a multi-coloured rainbow house, but we've really ran with that ethos,' Max adds. By 'we', he is referring to his friend, the designer and frame-maker Benedict Foley (see pages 22–31 for his cottage in Essex), who helped him to realise his vision for the house. 'Benedict was instrumental in turning my wild ideas into something that I wouldn't get bored of and that could stand the test of time,' Max says. 'I'm quite aware that treating an interior like a seasonal wardrobe would be illogical – it has to be a permanent collection!'

The house, although something of a wipe-clean white box when Max bought it, had good bones, giving them a canvas to tart up with paint and pattern. 'The idea of practicality fills me with horror and I decided right at the start to put my budget into the decoration rather than anything architectural or structural,' says Max. Little pediment-esque hats, whipped up by a carpenter to Benedict's design, were added to draw attention away from fairly standard doors, while upstairs, Max's bedroom door was painted with a red and blue serpentine

Max Hurd's library – a room he describes as 'calming but invigorating' – is a glossy green delight, painted in 'Sap Green' with woodwork in 'Bancha', both by Farrow & Ball. The slipper chair is upholstered in 'Leopard Stripe Green' from Sibyl Colefax & John Fowler, while the rug is by Campbell Rey for Nordic Knots.

shape inspired by one of Benedict's frames that he sells through his company A.Prin. In the kitchen, the existing units remained, but took on a rather different guise in Farrow & Ball's aptly named 'Fake Tan'. To distract from the fact that the wall cupboards were a couple of inches shy of the ceiling, Benedict suggested adding a crenellation detail to the top, inspired by Max's love of medieval castles. A built-in spice rack – a bit of practical kit that Max was adamant would have little other than salt on it under his guardianship – was adapted into a cork pinboard, which now accommodates a mishmash of letters and pictures. 'I love being surrounded by memories,' he says.

The front room – or the library, as Max refers to it on the basis that 'it has a few books in it' – is now a glossy green delight, painted in a combination of 'Sap Green' and 'Bancha' by Farrow & Ball, with a sofa upholstered in a green cotton velvet and laden with cushions made up from Sibyl Colefax & John Fowler and Décors Barbares fabrics. 'I knew exactly what I wanted from this room from the moment I set foot in the house,' Max explains. The adjoining drawing room-cum-bar proved more of a challenge. 'The builders were twiddling their thumbs, waiting for me to decide on the colour,' says Max, who eventually, thanks to Benedict's persuasive powers, settled on 'Bisque', a punchy orange from Farrow & Ball. 'I wanted pink and green, but Benedict wisely cautioned me that that combination had been done to death.' Max did win on the ceiling, though, which he had painted in sky blue after seeing it done in a palazzo in Venice. 'I love that it adds a grandeur, although Benedict did warn me that a Venetian palazzo has rather different ceilings to a two-bedroom worker's cottage in north London.'

While the house is full of wild flourishes, almost every element is underpinned by a narrative or the traditions of decoration. Max and Benedict pooled together references as diverse as a futuristic neon swimming pool by Verner Panton in Germany, which inspired the red and purple attic, to John Fowler-esque English country-house style, which features in everything from wall sconces and crystal-drop candlesticks to frilly blinds and pooled chintz curtains. 'My initial plan for the house was Oscar Wilde meets Marie Antoinette by way of

a Brazilian bordello,' Max explains. 'It's my favourite author, my favourite period of history and the country I grew up in, and weaving these stories together means the house is completely reflective of my personality.'

His bedroom, resplendent in orange and white stripes, was inspired by one of Max's favourite books, *Against Nature* by Joris-Karl Huysmans where the protagonist, after years of debauchery, found the only colour he could tolerate was orange. 'It's such a nice colour to wake up to,' Max says. The bed's headboard – an eBay find – is painted with a shell, a motif that is also repeated in the plaster scallop shell above the bed from which the bed canopy, made from Sibyl Colefax & John Fowler's 'Squiggle', hangs. 'It's *The Little Mermaid* meets John Fowler,' Max says, with a laugh. 'We took the values of English country-house decoration, but tried to give them a fun, contemporary twist,' he explains further. Equally, Max is a firm believer that if you love something, you will find a way to make it work in an interior. 'You can't be too obsessed with rules; it's about making a space that works for you,' he adds.

Although the house has a certain grandeur, Max is not the least bit precious. It started in his hands-on approach to decoration that saw him and Benedict – armed with a staple gun, a bit of wood, a stash of pins and a couple of glasses of champagne – fashioning things like the pink hall drapery. 'The whole place is basically held together with Blu-tack,' jokes Max. 'It wasn't about everything being up to an impeccable standard, but about creating a space that I could enjoy with friends,' he adds. 'I wanted it to be somewhere where they could relax. I'm not the least bit worried if something gets broken, and if it does, it automatically becomes my least favourite possession.' What Max and Benedict have created is a deeply liveable house, which manages to also inspire and amaze. 'It really sings for its supper – if you have guests, you can literally point them to a room and know that it will entertain them all evening,' Max says. 'It's great when you're tired.' Sadly, the doorbell will no longer be part of the entertainment, for it gave up the ghost a few months after I visited. Thank goodness the rest remains.

THE LITTLE BLACK JACKET CARINE ROITFELD

Carine Roitfeld irreverent

Benedict Foley, who worked with Max on the decoration of his house, cautioned against a trendy pale pink for the drawing room; instead they opted for Farrow & Ball's warming yet punchy 'Bisque'. The antique table to the right was one of the first pieces that Max bought for the house.

The existing kitchen units remained, but
were painted, along with the walls, in Farrow
& Ball's brilliantly named 'Fake Tan'. The
under-cupboard curtains were made from
Sibyl Colefax & John Fowler's 'Tea Pots'
fabric, a discontinued design, which Max
begged the brand to sell him a roll of.

A theatrical pink ballgown-esque curtain
hangs in the hallway, framing the view
into Max's bedroom, which is papered in
Farrow & Ball's 'Tented Stripe' in orange.
The headboard was an eBay find, while the
canopy and curtains are both made from
Sibyl Colefax & John Fowler's 'Squiggle'.

The wardrobe was a £40 steal from eBay, which Max papered himself with end-of-roll leftovers from the walls. Upstairs, the attic is painted in Farrow & Ball's 'Blazer', while the sofa is upholstered in a linen by plaster artist Viola Lanari.

ROSI DE RUIG

Lampshade maker, Dorset

For Rosi de Ruig, the lampshade maker known for her colourful shades and glossy lacquer table lamps, her house in the rolling chalky hills of west Dorset has grown alongside her business. 'As I gained confidence with my work, I became more confident with how I decorated this house,' says Rosi, who founded her company in 2015. 'I would never have painted this room green when we bought the house almost 10 years ago, but through my lampshades, I've become more comfortable using layers of colour and being a bit bolder,' she says, referring to the apple-green kitchen, which looks out over the garden to the hills beyond. 'It didn't come to me until after we'd painted it, but I realise the colour was hugely inspired by the landscape around us,' she adds. 'It's an inspiring place to be.'

Rosi and her husband were looking for a weekend escape from their busy lives in west London where they could enjoy greener pastures with their three children. 'The contrast to where we live in Shepherd's Bush is comical, really,' says Rosi. 'The children have such freedom here.' Originally, they were looking for a bolthole closer to London, but once they discovered this part of west Dorset – a place Rosi describes as a 'beautiful wilderness' – they found themselves committed to finding a house there. This one, the former stables to the larger house next door, had been on the market for

a couple of years, but prospective buyers were put off by the fact that it was higgledy-piggledy and crudely converted. Rosi, however, saw its merits. 'It felt wonderfully secluded on the edge of a village, but what really enchanted us were the nice bright, light rooms,' she explains. 'We're a tall family, and we fell for its wonderful head height.'

Still, the fact remained that it was going to be a huge project, and Rosi and her husband put a lot of initial energy into rationalising the space. A glass link was added to join the main stone house to a barn, providing space for an extra bedroom and all of the back-of-house spaces like utility rooms and a loo. In the main part of the house, the sitting room was extended at the back, creating a larger bedroom for Rosi above and making the most of the views, while a 'glorified ladder' was replaced by an elegant staircase that connects the living quarters to four bedrooms and two bathrooms. The big layout changes happened in a fairly concentrated fashion, but Rosi wanted to add colour and layers at a more leisurely pace. 'I like to decorate in phases,' she explains. 'I knew I wanted to create an interesting and playful home, and bring in some warmth and softness through colour.' She was also at pains to respect the space's origins. 'It's not a grand house, and I hated the idea of creating something that felt fancy,' she says. 'I wanted to do what felt right for a house in Dorset that was originally a stable.'

Rosi and her husband bought their west Dorset house, a converted stables, 10 years ago, enchanted by its light, bright rooms and the beautiful landscape within which it sits. They added a glass link between the main stone house and a barn to create an extra bedroom and back-of-house space.

As Rosi's lampshades prove, she has a wonderful understanding of colour and how to combine it. 'In the house, it was about using colour in a way that was both restful and invigorating,' she explains. 'I think that if you can get the balance of colour and pattern right, it will have such a huge impact on the space.' As such, the lively green of the kitchen, with its pink and red zig-zag pattern curtains, is tempered by the soft yellow hallway, papered in Nicholas Herbert's 'Celestria' wallpaper, onto which it leads. Off from this is the equally soothing sitting room. The walls are painted in Edward Bulmer's 'Cuisse de Nymphe Emue', and a large pastel by artist Oisin Byrne hangs, as if made specially for the spot, above the fireplace. 'We bought the artwork in May in the mad hot days of that first lockdown,' recalls Rosi. 'This room used to be sky blue, but it felt quite cold, so we repainted it pink in lockdown and it feels so calm now.' For Rosi, this is all part of the decorating process. 'It takes time to establish the relationship between oneself and your home,' Rosi says. 'I will ask myself "Have I let that room down?" and then maybe I'll make some changes to rectify. I guess that is what is so liberating about paint – it is relatively easy to change.'

Bold decorative flourishes weave their way throughout, often in the form of a rug or, unsurprisingly, one of Rosi's decorative paper lampshades. 'Sometimes I put a lampshade in a room and end up tweaking the room accordingly,' she admits. 'More often than not, the shades are the perfect way to introduce pattern into a room.' Sometimes, patterns are given a little more prominence, as is the case in the space at the far end of the sitting room, which is kitted out with bookshelves and a sweet bar area papered in a red-and-white recycled cotton paper from Craft Boat in Jaipur, which Rosi often uses for her lampshades. 'It wouldn't have worked for a whole room, but it looks wonderful here,' she says, having paired it with navy woodwork and jolly red-and-white striped curtains. Stripes are a firm favourite, also cropping up in the small stables opposite the main house, where Rosi had them painted onto the ceiling. 'It was totally inspired by Gavin Houghton's sitting room in Morocco, and I'd definitely do it again if another ceiling presented itself,' she says, laughing.

The upstairs rooms in the main house are quieter, but no less joyful. 'We often turn up after a long week and hours in the car, and I just wanted these rooms to feel as peaceful as possible,' she explains. In her bedroom, she opted for a delicate wallpaper from Anna Jeffreys, which she also used in the yellow colourway in the ensuite bathroom and paired with patterned tiles from Milagros. The children's bathroom, while still calm, is a little livelier, adorned with a star-bedecked wallpaper by Molly Mahon and a sweet antique cabinet that Rosi had fashioned into a vanity. 'I found lots for the house at antiques fairs, as we didn't arrive with much,' she explains. 'Bridport is nearby and is a wonderful source of antiques, so we've swapped out poorly painted broken furniture for better things over the years.'

Did the fact this wasn't her main home change her approach to decorating? 'I guess it gave me the licence to be a bit more playful, as it didn't need to be as hard-working as our London house,' Rosi suggests. 'I didn't want it to be annoying or silly, but I did want to give the space a gentle energy.' That, she most certainly has.

The hallway – papered in Nicholas Herbert's
soft yellow 'Celestria' wallpaper – leads into the
drawing room. The walls in here are painted in
'Cuisse de Nymphe Emue' by Edward Bulmer,
with a large pastel by artist Oisin Byrne hanging
above the fireplace, which was made by local
craftsman Jasper Shackleton.

At the far end of the sitting room is a bar and library area, with woodwork painted in a bespoke blue, and the bar splashback papered in a red-and-white recycled cotton paper from Craft Boat in Jaipur. The kitchen walls are painted in 'Raw Tomatillo' by Farrow & Ball, with stainless steel units from IKEA and curtains from Tinsmiths.

Rosi's bedroom is papered in 'Laurel Overlay
Green Rose' from Anna Jeffreys, while the
bathroom is in Molly Mahon's 'Spot and Star'
wallpaper, with an antique cabinet that has
been turned into a vanity. A small stable building
was converted into a sitting room and office
space, with the stripes on the ceiling inspired
by those in Gavin Houghton's house in Morocco.

MARK HOMEWOOD

Buyer, Somerset

Mark Homewood is one of those people whose taste manages to be both incredibly broad and just so. As illustrated at his sixteenth-century red sandstone farmhouse in Somerset, his is a world where exuberant royal icing-esque plasterwork, folk art chairs, a Calder-esque mobile and a contemporary modular sofa coalesce in happy harmony. 'I've always loved that mix of contemporary and vintage, probably because it's what I've done for years at work,' explains Mark, who as head of buying and retail at Designers Guild has spent the best part of three decades sourcing products. 'We could have gone down the minimal or the traditional route here, but I guess what we've tried to do is bridge the two,' explains Mark, who bought the house with his partner, the costume designer Michael Sharp, in 2018. 'I'm too much of a hoarder for it ever to have been minimal, so what we have tried to do is make it look like it had evolved over a long time. I wanted it to feel a bit eccentric.'

Before they moved to Gaulden Manor, Mark and Michael had been living in a Georgian house about an hour away. 'I put off coming to see this house for a while, because I knew what would happen once I did,' recalls Mark, with a knowing grin. It is not hard to see why the couple fell for the farmhouse: it has charm in spades and is tucked away from everything, surrounded by gardens and fields. 'You don't know you are here until you are right on top of it,' Mark explains. The house itself is laced with history: a dwelling has been recorded on the site since the twelfth century, but this farmhouse dates back to the sixteenth century, with some seventeenth-century additions, including the remarkable plasterwork in the Great Hall and the smaller Chapel off it, which was dreamed up by its then owner James Turbeville, the Bishop of Exeter – a Catholic in hiding from Protestant Queen Elizabeth I – as a way to celebrate his life. 'I love that this daft plasterwork was added to jazz up what started out as a modest farmhouse,' says Mark, pointing out motifs ranging from James Turbeville's coat of arms to pomegranates and, at the more macabre end of the spectrum, skeletons.

Aside from the fairly precise plasterwork, the house is full of wonky charm, which Mark and Michael were keen to embrace. 'I can't bear old places when they've been given sharp edges,' Mark admits. 'I never understand why houses that have been through hundreds of years of use are given facelifts that rip out all of their softness and romance.' The layout stayed largely the same too, mainly because the house is Grade II* listed, but also because it worked well – with a small kitchen, dining room, study, and larger Great Hall and Chapel on the ground floor, and five bedrooms and three bathrooms upstairs. The only real change was to swap the dining room and kitchen around.

In the Great Hall, seventeenth century royal icing-esque plasterwork provides a backdrop to Hay's green modular 'Mags' sofa, a green PVC cord side table by Marni and a multi-coloured mid-century metal floor lamp.

Although unintentional, the newly positioned kitchen has something of Charleston Farmhouse in Sussex about it, with an inglenook fireplace and cupboards pieced together from an old haberdashery unit that Mark found in the south of France. 'It wasn't a conscious reference, but I guess Charleston was a big influence on the house, and this room has a sort of crafted feel,' he explains. The pink and black walls – in fact, some of the very few in the house to be painted a colour – add to this feeling. 'I've used this pink – it's 'Cinder Rose' by Farrow & Ball – a lot over the years, and it just really works,' explains Mark. 'Pinks, purples and greens worked really well in this house,' he adds, pointing out the green and white hallway, which the couple have clad in reclaimed tongue-and-groove. What did not sit so well was blue. 'It's one of my favourite colours, but I just couldn't make it work in the countryside,' he explains. As such, the navy blue Great Hall walls that they inherited soon became white. 'Every colour we considered for this room just distracted the eye away from the plasterwork above, so in the end we went with white,' he says.

Blue may not have worked for the walls, but it certainly comes in through things – the embroidered quilt on Mark and Michael's bed, the blue and white floral wallpaper that enlivens one of their bathrooms, and the Delft tiles that provide a charming splashback for the Aga in the kitchen. In fact, most of the colour in the house comes in through the pieces furnishing it. The white walls of the Great Hall provide a foil to colourful pieces, including a pair of 1940s armchairs by Otto Shultz in a yellow cotton from Designers Guild, a green modular 'Mags' Hay sofa, a vintage rag rug and a multi-coloured mid-century metal floor lamp. 'I love colour, but I liked the idea of adding it through pieces that we could swap in and out,' Mark explains. 'We never wanted to create a house that was fixed in aspic.' That, of course, and the fact that a flexible approach allows for the fruits of sourcing trips to continue to find their way into the space.

What makes the farmhouse feel exciting is the way pieces are combined. There might be a nostalgic floral, but then there

is also a vivid green Marni side table made from PVC cord. 'I like the juxtaposition of something traditional that has been around for years, with a hit of something modern,' explains Mark. The curtains in his bedroom illustrate this point well: they are made mainly from a vintage fabric adorned with pheasants, with a neon-green strip of Designers Guild linen forming the outer edge. 'The vintage curtains came from a house we used to have in France but weren't quite big enough, so we added the linen,' explains Mark, who continued the green theme with a vintage chest of drawers and pillows on the bed. 'I love how the linen gives the curtains a contemporary shot.' It is a recurring combination in the house, also playing out in the Chapel, where an old Chesterfield sofa – upholstered in a botanical print from John Derian – and a traditional Georgian console are paired with a green floral 1970s rug, a zingy pink Marni chair and a Calder-esque kinetic mobile that gently sways overhead. 'For me, this kind of mix is what gives rooms energy,' Mark explains.

What Mark and Michael have conjured up through their thoughtful decoration is the feeling of a house that has developed over a much longer period than the five years they have been there. Did it all just naturally come together or did they plan out the rooms? 'It all started in quite a calculated way, but that discipline fell off the edge of a cliff quite quickly,' admits Mark who often rents the space out as a location house and runs his own online shop selling vintage and antique finds. 'I'm just always getting seduced by things.' This also accounts for why Mark, at one point, was moving house every couple of years, living in spaces as diverse as Shoreditch loft conversions, Georgian houses and everything in between. 'I was always getting new ideas through work and always wanting to do something different,' he explains. 'But this place feels like a synthesis of all of that and I'm happier here than anywhere we've ever lived, both in terms of the setting and also what we've ended up with visually.' Long may it last. Although, I suspect this one may continue to happily evolve, as all good interiors should.

At the other end of the Great Hall, an MDF
Italia table contrasts with a pair of painted
antique folk chairs and ceramic vessels by
Dutch industrial designer Hella Jongerius.
The chapel is just off the Great Hall, and
features an old Chesterfield sofa, upholstered
in a botanical print from John Derian, a Calder-
esque kinetic mobile and a 1970s floral rug.

The kitchen is painted in 'Cinder Rose'
by Farrow & Ball, which is one of Mark's
favourite pinks. Mark had the kitchen made
from an old haberdashery unit he found in
the south of France, while the splashback
is made from antique Delft tiles.

A Victorian English four-poster bed takes
centre stage in Mark's bedroom, with curtains
made from a vintage patterned fabric and
a neon green strip of Designers Guild fabric.
A woven chair by Moroso adds a contemporary
flourish and picks up the green. The painting
of the jug came from the south of France.

In the otherwise white bathroom, a splash of colour comes from the Designers Guild wallpaper, the boucherouite rug and antique Swedish seaweed print. The house itself is a sixteenth-century red sandstone farmhouse, which has been added to over the years.

CATH KIDSTON

Designer, west London

If the name Cath Kidston brings to mind nostalgic rosebuds and pink polka dots, her house in west London may come as a bit of a shock: floral prints are in short supply; the walls – bar a couple of exceptions – are in relatively neutral tones; and colour, while most certainly there, finds form in considered bursts. 'The house has pattern and colour, but not in the most obvious way,' says Cath. 'Decoration for me is about the mix – a bit of old furniture, pictures, a little bit of print layered in, as well as plants. Always plants,' she adds. I'm a one-trick pony, really.' I have to disagree, for she has plenty of tricks up her sleeve, not least the two new businesses she has launched since leaving her eponymous brand in 2016 – C.Atherley, a body care and fragrance brand, which grew out of her long-term love affair with scented geraniums, and a print studio called Joy of Print. 'My mind is always editing and I needed somewhere to channel all of my ideas for prints,' she says with a grin.

Pattern and print are what makes Cath tick. 'I've collected prints ever since I worked for Nicky Haslam when I was in my twenties,' she recalls. 'Once you get into it, print is like a language. I'm hopeless at remembering important facts, but I can vividly recall the stripy rosebud fabric and lilac walls of my childhood home.' At her own house, print and colour take shape in pockets that range from swirly pink-and-red lampshades in the sitting room to the delicate yellow-and-white seaweed wallpaper that lines the walls of her husband Hugh's bedroom. Print is never used superfluously, but in a way that feels measured and thoughtful. 'I like patterns all the more for their contrast with plain elements in rooms,' she adds, citing her bedroom as an example where soft pink walls offset pretty floral print bed-drapes, a squiggly pink-and-brown patterned rug and green striped blinds. 'I like a taste of pattern rather than being swamped by it.'

Cath bought this classic four-storey Edwardian terrace in 2017, attracted by its magical communal gardens and the fact it had not been modernised. 'We wanted to make our own thing, so it was heaven to find something like this,' explains Cath, who lives here during the week and spends weekends at their house in Gloucestershire. 'I've done up so many houses like this over the years and I knew we could make something of it,' she says. The biggest intervention was moving the kitchen from the basement to the raised ground floor, which became one large room that now runs the depth of the house, and also contains a dining table and seating area. 'It was a totally pivotal change because it somehow just opened up the whole house,' she says. The basement was extended by 3 metres at the rear, creating space for a terrace above, and now accommodates a lovely large sitting room, as well as a laundry room, study

The basement hallway is painted in Farrow & Ball's 'Picture Gallery Red' in satin, with a Swedish rag rug runner underfoot. Just glimpsed is the laundry room ahead and a little loo to the right, which is papered in Howe at 36 Bourne Street's 'Knurl' in brick.

and small loo. Perhaps controversially, in a world where we are always squeezing in extra bedrooms, Cath decided to reduce them to just two – one for her and one for her husband, giving each their own floor and accompanying bathroom.

Rather like the layout changes, the decoration was something of a jigsaw puzzle. There was the fact that Cath was forced to plan most of it remotely from Gloucestershire, due to the lockdown, as well as the fact that beloved possessions from their previous house naturally governed how rooms came together. And then there was the fact that parts of the house presented a challenge when it came to introducing colour. 'The kitchen goes straight into the staircase, so the colour I chose for that would need to go all the way up to the top floor,' explains Cath, who eventually settled on a warm off-white that works beautifully throughout. 'The first shade we tried ended up looking green, so we had to repaint the whole room,' she confesses. 'But that's what happens when you have to choose paints from a studio in Gloucestershire.'

While the off-white may in itself not be remarkable, the kitchen and staircase really came into their own when Cath added the next piece to the jigsaw: art. 'I have a picture addiction,' she admits. 'I just bought a small picture of geraniums and I've got no clue where I'm going to put it. I guess I see pictures as very similar to pattern and print – they are a bridge between contemporary and traditional, and play a huge part in creating mood in an interior.' Much of the art in the house – especially the prints and botanical works adorning Cath's bathroom, and the paintings and prints in the hallway – came from Cath's previous house. Some new pieces were bought for specific spots too, including the abstract Ellsworth Kelly that now hangs above the fireplace next to the dining table. 'That tomato-red is one of my favourite colours,' she says. 'It sets the tone for the whole space,' she adds.

Red is a tone used in abundance throughout the house. There is the punchy red stool in the kitchen, for instance, which enlivens the Carrara marble and Douglas fir. Then there is the majestic poppy-red four-poster bed in Cath's bedroom – a 'crazy lockdown choice' which, in fact, completely makes the room. 'I am so happy with it,' says Cath, who picked up the tone in the ric rac trim on the bedside lamps and the tasselled fringe on the bed drapes. 'I love how it gives things a pop.' Downstairs, in the basement hallway, she has used the colour to create a little more than a burst, painting every inch of the space, including the joinery, in a rich terracotta. She picked up the tone in the little loo off this space, too, papering the walls in Howe's geometric-adorned 'Knurl' paper. 'I'm a total wallpaper freak, but I like it in limited ways,' she explains. The only other room it crops up in is Hugh's bedroom on the top floor, where a twig-like wallpaper – in fact one of Cath's own designs for Joy of Print, called 'Coral' – provides a calm backdrop for a lemon-yellow chest of drawers and a patchwork quilt.

The most colourful room, however, is the basement sitting room. Here, colour comes not from the off-white walls but from the pieces layered up in the space – an abstract pink-and-white rug, a pair of purple armchairs with pink American blankets draped over the back, a floral tablecloth made from Cath's own Joy of Print 'Coral' design, a sofa upholstered in a print by Peggy Angus, and art that includes a joyful pastel by contemporary artist Oisin Byrne (his work also features in Rosi de Ruig's house, pages 112–121) and prints by British Op Art artist Michael Kidner. 'It's this kind of combination that I naturally gravitate to when putting rooms together,' says Cath, who credits growing up in the countryside as one of the key influences on the way she decorates. 'Layers are what gives a place atmosphere and warmth.' I couldn't agree more.

In the basement living area, a work by artist Oisin Byrne takes centre stage, with its colours picked up by a Rosi de Ruig lampshade, a Robert Stephenson rug and a table covered in Joy of Print's 'Coral' fabric in grass. The purple chairs are antique covered in velvet from George Spencer, with old American blankets from Clive Rogers hanging over the back.

In the open-plan kitchen and dining area on the
ground floor, walls painted in 'Joanna' by Little
Greene provide a calming backdrop, while an
abstract piece by Ellsworth Kelly, along with
a Robert Stephenson rug and a stool in the
kitchen provide pops of Cath's favourite shade
of red. The kitchen is made from Douglas fir.

The poppy-red four-poster bed in Cath's bedroom was made by Colin Orchard, with drapes made from Lisa Fine's 'Samode' linen in poppy. The ensuite walls are lined with art, including a watercolour of tulips by artist Rory McEwen. The chair is an antique that Cath found in Tetbury.

JORGE PEREZ-MARTIN & DAVID GIBSON

Antiques dealers, Gloucestershire

'N othing is off limits' is a phrase antiques dealers Jorge Perez-Martin and David Gibson often use when describing the sorts of pieces they source for Brownrigg, their renowned Tetbury antiques shop. But it is a mantra that is equally applicable to the renovation of the couple's house, a dreamy limestone villa that sits handsomely on the side of a green and hilly valley not far from Stroud. For this is a renovation that has evolved over eight years and – given Jorge and David's enthusiasm – it could well continue for as long as they live there. Parts of the house are as close as they will ever come to being finished, and some parts are still a long way off. 'We're in it for the long haul,' says David, with a smile. The only thing that was strictly off-limits was taking everything back to bare bones and starting afresh. 'We wanted to preserve the building's history,' says Jorge, speaking like a true antiques dealer. The pair are at pains to respect the soul of the house and to allow it to develop slowly around the pieces they collect – everything from a nineteenth-century cast-iron bathtub, with a distinctive zinc canopy, to an eighteenth-century chinoiserie bureau and terracotta flooring found in Serbia.

The couple bought the house 10 years ago, well aware of the labour of love that they were about to embark on. The house was a bit of a warren, with an early eighteenth-century core and nineteenth-century additions (including a small family chapel), as well as a 1960s extension that was something of a blight on the eastern side of the property. But the bones were good, with an elegant 1830s late Regency part giving the house a quiet grandeur and accommodating the formal rooms, including the drawing room and dining room on the ground floor, and bedrooms, a dressing room and bathroom above. Right at the start, Jorge and David decided they would not tinker with the room sizes, and so other than turning a few existing rooms into bathrooms, they have worked with the layout they inherited. Walls were stripped, revealing past schemes that were left in all of their distressed and peeling glory. 'It's these scars that give the house such soul and patina,' says David, who recalls having to often ask the builders to stop midway through their work when just the right amount of original paint had been unearthed. That, of course, is the benefit of living on-site through a renovation project, rather than taking shelter elsewhere.

The jarring 1960s add-on was demolished and the gaping hole left in the side of the house filled with an expansive glass wall that now floods the library with light. This room is filled with some of David and Jorge's favourite pieces and is one of the few in the house to have white walls – although if the gentle bickering that feeds their creative process is anything to go by, I sense this could be due a change in the coming years. The colour and the texture in here come in through

One of the few white rooms in the house, colour here comes from an array of decorative objects and furniture, including a Spanish 1960s faux malachite ceramic column, an early nineteenth-century giltwork mirror and sheepskin armchairs by Danish designer Birte Iversen.

treasured furniture, antiques and decorative objects, collected over the past 30 or so years – a green faux malachite 1960s column, an ornate early nineteenth-century gilded mirror, a pair of sheepskin armchairs by Danish designer Birte Iversen, and framed twentieth-century seaweed specimens. It is a diverse collection, but then that is what Brownrigg – which was founded over 25 years ago – is all about. 'We liked the idea of this room being quite modern and crisp,' explains Jorge. 'But we're also pretty brave when it comes to using colour,' adds David, accounting for why much of the house is a feast of vibrant patterns and rich tones. 'We chose colour palettes in a way that most good decorators would be horrified by, taking each room separately and not thinking too much about the house as a whole,' David explains. I think this is perhaps a bit of good English modesty, because the rooms have a wonderful sense of flow, taking you on a journey from the unexpected to the sheer joyful.

A vaulted twin bedroom falls somewhere between the two: plush and jewel-like, and papered in the raspberry-toned 'Pine' – a design by their friends, local wallpaper and fabric brand Whiteworks. 'The paper kicked the whole room off,' explains Jorge. Soon followed the antique brass and chrome twin beds, which the couple bought eight years before: they stripped off the glossy white paint, polished them up and cloaked them in green velvet. A mid-twentieth-century Spanish painting found the perfect spot above the fireplace, while a pair of hand-painted lampshades by Alvaro Picardo knit all the layers together. 'I loved the fact that the English country house is traditionally so eclectic, and we wanted to embrace that,' says Jorge, who moved from Spain to England when he was in his early twenties. Sitting in the corner is a key country-house ingredient – a Howard & Sons armchair, which Jorge had reupholstered in Carolina Irving's blue and gold 'Paisley Velvet'. 'Sometimes I'd just like to come for a little thinking time in here,' says Jorge. Next door is a candy-pink bathroom. 'I think I just got on with that without telling Jorge,' jokes David. 'Yes, it's a colour I would have found way too girly a few years ago, but I love how bright it feels,' Jorge admits.

Pattern plays a big part in the house's decoration. For an attic bedroom, they opted for a yellow check for the walls and ceiling, and papered the adjoining bathroom in Gastón y Daniela's vivid 'Papel Pintado Amazonia Original', a paper that Jorge had had his eye on for a few years. It is a brave, but perfectly executed choice, which at first might seem quite punchy but soon feels very soothing thanks to the nineteenth-century zinc bath, antique washstand and mustard armchair invitingly positioned in the corner. 'We tried to do every room like it was our own bedroom,' Jorge explains. 'No guest should feel as if they have been allocated the duff bedroom and we wanted them to feel they had a space to escape to for some me-time,' adds David. 'The thing with this house: it might feel quite large, but we have tried to design it in a way so that we still use all of it on a regular basis.' Greens feature prominently throughout the house, cropping up in the kitchen and pantry, and on the walls of the downstairs loo, which is papered in 'Hunters', another jolly design from Whiteworks. It's eccentric and quintessentially English, transforming the miniscule space into something quite magical. Equally transfixing is a green guest bedroom, where a wall of distressed original paint, exposed by the builders, sets a palette that includes Farrow & Ball's 'Saxon Green', handstitched cushions from Paula Bailie and 'Coral' wallpaper from Cath Kidston's Joy of Print. 'That paper reminds me of the sea at home and I knew we'd use it somewhere the moment I first saw it,' explains Jorge.

In other rooms, specific antiques, unsurprisingly, guided how the decoration would evolve. Jorge and David are not the sort to immediately head to a conventional bathroom supplier, and so it was something of a waiting game when it came to sourcing a bath. The fact they had to get Listed Building Consent to create a bathroom in one of the loveliest rooms at the front of the house bought them some time, and a few years into the renovation, just the bath came along – a spectacular nineteenth-century cast-iron bath with a zinc canopy by Doulton. 'That was the starting point for the whole room and pushed us to create something really special,' Jorge explains. They called on specialist decorative painter Magdalena Gordon to work her magic; she set up camp for weeks, coating the walls in a delicious red tortoiseshell inspired by a seventeenth-century bargueño desk and turning the ceiling into a coffered *trompe l'oeil* spectacle. 'I didn't want something that we'd seen in so many magazines,' Jorge explains. 'It would never have been part of our plan in our first year here, but it takes patience for rooms to come together,' adds David. 'It's also the benefit of not trying to make decisions about decoration at the same time as thinking about replacing a roof or making structural changes, when things like tortoiseshell walls might seem like a silly indulgence.' The bathroom now serves the dual purpose of a snug little sitting room and has something of the Grand Tour about it, with an assortment of marble urns and columns, an eighteenth-century English mahogany library chair, a nineteenth-century French Empire Gueridon table and a terrific Art Deco bronze chandelier.

Both Jorge and David admit that their house is an exercise in patience. 'We've really tried not to compromise,' David says. This is a house built around the things that fill it – pieces, as all dealers and collectors will know, that cannot be found at the click of a mouse but take time to come along. It is considered decoration at its very best, where no detail has been overlooked and where rooms have been allowed to evolve bit by bit, rather than being the work of a rushed renovation. It's precisely how it should be and the privilege that they feel at being part of it is palpable.

Greens weave throughout the house, including in the kitchen, with its La Cornue cooker and Italian eighteenth century tiles. The salt and pepper grinders and egg stand are from Bath-based design shop Berdoulat. The downstairs loo is papered in 'Hunters' by Whiteworks.

Papered in 'Pine' by Whiteworks, the guest
bedroom features a pair of antique brass
and chrome beds, with green velvet drapes.
The Spanish painting above the fireplace
is mid-twentieth-century, while the
lampshades are by Alvaro Picardo. An
attic guest bathroom is papered in Gastón y
Daniela's 'Papel Pintado Amazonia Original'.

The main bathroom features a nineteenth century cast iron bath by Doulton; the red tortoiseshell walls and coffered *trompe l'oeil* ceiling are the work of specialist decorative painter Magdalena Gordon. A wall of distressed original paint, unearthed by the builders, set the palette for this guest bedroom, with the fireplace painted in Farrow & Ball's 'Saxon Green'.

MARY GRAHAM

Interior designer, North Yorkshire

Mary Graham is one half of Salvesen Graham, the London-based interior design studio known for its fresh take on English country-house style. Colour, patterned fabrics and gathered lampshades are a mainstay in their projects, as are squishy sofas, ruffled blinds and frilly-edged cushions. 'We want our interiors to feel rooted in tradition, but with a forward-thinking, contemporary twist,' explains Mary. 'A lot of what we do is about nostalgia – for some people it is a bit of an old-fashioned idea, but for us it conjures up happy memories, home and, crucially, comfort,' she adds. 'That's exactly what something like a frilly skirt on a sofa does for me.'

Frilly skirts run riot at Mary's own six-bedroom farmhouse in North Yorkshire, cropping up not just on sofas, but also on bed valances, on a sweet floral slipper chair in Mary's bathroom and even on the under-counter curtains in the boot room. In fact, the only room not to have one is the olive-green dining room. 'I just love the femininity of them, although I hadn't realised quite how much they had wielded their way into my own house,' says Mary. Unsurprisingly, her home plays host to many more decorative flourishes that have become synonymous with Salvesen Graham – from the painted chequerboard floor in the family room to the floral fabric-laden half-tester in Mary's bedroom. 'Our house is less a testing ground and more somewhere that I've decided to employ my favourite elements from our projects,' explains Mary. 'I see these things so much at work, so it's nice to live with old friends around you.'

Mary moved from London to Yorkshire with her husband, Sam, and two young children in 2019. 'It was always part of the plan that we'd end up here,' says Mary of the farmhouse, which belongs to Sam's family and sits half a mile down a bumpy track from his parents. 'It had been tenanted for a long time, so I'd only ever seen it from a distance on a rainy walk.' It was only when Mary and Sam got the keys in 2018 that she realised quite what she was getting herself into: 'There was rising damp, mouldy walls and lots of bleak rooms,' she recalls. And so, faced with rather a larger task than anticipated, the couple set to work. The flow and proportions worked well, thanks to the fact that the house is basically a square, so the layout stayed pretty much the same, with the exception of the attic, which they opened up to create two bedrooms and a bathroom. A screen of leylandii trees were taken down, opening up the views and bringing light into the rear of the house, while a crumbling lean-to was replaced by an extension – created in collaboration with architect Rupert Cunningham, from Ben Pentreath's studio – that now accommodates the wonderfully light family room, as well as the boot room and loo.

Once the bones were in order, a few favourite fabrics kickstarted the decoration. Before the kitchen had even started to take shape, a cheerful floral – Le Manach's 'Palmyre' – was destined for the flouncy blinds, which elevate the room to something well beyond a place for whipping up lunch. 'I loved the idea of using an extravagant fabric in here that you might usually expect in a drawing room, because it's the space we spend the most time in,' explains Mary, who added an acid lemon trim to give the fabric a modern punch. Farrow & Ball's 'Archive No. 227' was carefully chosen to match the ground colour of the fabric, while she opted for simple units that are topped with white marble. 'I wanted it to provide a calm backdrop for busy family life,' explains Mary. In spite of her own dislike for islands, she designed one for the centre of the room, popping it on legs so that it is more of a table, and giving it playful curved edges. 'We needed storage and if there is anything I love more than frilly skirts, it is practicality,' says Mary.

A less practical, though totally perfect, choice was Jean Monro's 'Mansfield' fabric, which takes centre stage in the drawing room and answers all of Mary's dreams for a blowsy chintz sofa. 'I don't let people sit on it if they're drinking red wine,' she says, with a grin. 'It's the only thing I'm precious about.' Again, the fabric – festooned with hollyhocks, roses and tulips – set the tone for the entire room, with walls in Edward Bulmer's 'Jonquil', a pink Turkish flatweave rug from Robert Stephenson, and a sofa in Claremont's 'Cunard' fabric in the aubergine colourway. In a similar way, she had her heart set on a lively multi-toned floral fabric – 'Dans la Florêt' from Décor Barbares – for the gathered under-counter skirt in the boot room. 'The fabric is far too fancy for a boot room, but it gives me immense pleasure,' admits Mary, who meticulously calculated the quantity of material required and used the minimal leftovers for a trim elsewhere. 'I felt a bit like I was at the butcher's, trying to work out a way to get the most out of a joint of meat,' she says, with a laugh.

Much of the house, in fact, was about balancing decorative fantasies and flourishes with creative compromises. 'It pushed me to think a bit differently, because we didn't have the budget for all the lovely things that we usually use for clients,' Mary explains. As such, a favourite paisley from de Le Cuona was limited to the window-seat cushion and curtain heading in the drawing room, while the curtains in here were made from a plain chocolate-brown linen. 'There is something nice about not having your favourite fabric in the most obvious

spot,' observes Mary. Similarly, in the olive-green dining room, a favourite – and rather indulgent – Claremont pattern was restricted to the window-seat cushion. 'I'd usually think about using it for the curtains, but we couldn't stretch to that,' explains Mary, who instead opted for a plain linen and tricked them up with a pink leading trim. 'It just makes them feel a bit more elevated,' she adds. 'I'd never usually dream of plain curtains, so it's a good lesson in thinking beyond my first idea.'

For all of the colour and pattern in the house, there are also quieter spaces, including the green and white family room off the kitchen, which looks like something out of New England, with off-white tongue-and-groove-clad walls and a pitched roof. 'Our friends were really surprised that I'd gone for white, but it just makes the most of the fact that this room is filled with light,' Mary explains. 'The colours really pop on top of it,' she adds, pointing out the green and white painted chequerboard floor and the floral fabric – Salvesen Graham's own 'Floral Trail' – on the sofas. 'I limited myself with the palette, but it proves how a room can still feel layered without using lots of different colours and patterns.' Mary's own bedroom also sits at the more restrained end of the spectrum, with walls in Farrow & Ball's 'String', curtains in Jean Monro's 'Bowness' chintz, and a half-tester bed made up from Salvesen Graham's own 'Floral Sprig' voile. 'I designed this room exactly the opposite way that I would for a client, as we painted the walls first and then found fabrics that would work,' Mary explains. 'The Jean Monro is a gentle pattern but says a lot to me.' In fact, the whole room says a lot – the combination of prints and colours may be subtle, but there is an overwhelming sense of calm, especially in the fading afternoon light. 'It's the room you see day in, day out, so it has to be restful,' Mary stresses. 'I always tell clients that guest rooms are where you should indulge any decorative fantasies.'

If the charming twin bedroom in the attic is anything to go by, Mary has certainly taken heed of that advice. Salvesen Graham's own 'Floral Sprig' wallpaper climbs up the walls and ceiling, while a pair of properly made beds with blankets, mustard headboards and wonderful floral valances look like something out of a children's story book. 'I guess it goes back to nostalgia,' says Mary. 'I wanted it to feel like the sort of room I might have stayed in when I was a child; it was about creating something deeply comforting that immediately conjures up that feeling of home.'

Walls in Edward Bulmer's 'Jonquil' and a fireplace
painted in Farrow & Ball's 'Bancha' provide a
sophisticated backdrop to the drawing room.
The sofa is upholstered in Jean Monro's 'Mansfield',
while the green floral chair is part of Salvesen
Graham's collaboration with David Seyfried and
is covered in 'Grace' in cyan by Jasper. The dining
room is painted in Sanderson's 'Oxney Olive'.

The kitchen is painted in Farrow & Ball's 'Archive' with a splashback in 'Felce' tiles from Balineum. Opposite this is an extension, which now accommodates a wonderfully light family room. The green checkerboard floor was inspired by something similar Mary had done in a project. The sofa is upholstered in Salvesen Graham's own 'Floral Trail'.

Salvesen Graham's 'Floral Sprig' wallpaper provides a calming backdrop to the twin guest bedroom. Mary's ensuite bathroom features woodwork painted in Farrow & Ball's 'Sap Green' and walls in Sanderson's 'Truffle' wallpaper. The main bedroom features walls in Farrow & Ball's 'String' and curtains in Jean Monro's 'Bowness' chintz.

TOBIAS VERNON

Interior designer and gallerist, Somerset

What is remarkable about this cottage in the picture-perfect village of Mells, in Somerset, is the way in which a jewel-like interior has been conjured up when the walls are painted in Dulux white. That, of course, is down to the skill of its custodian, the curator and interior designer Tobias Vernon, who has filled the two-up two-down space with a spattering of art and furniture so diverse that it sees a Sandra Blow screen print, an Orkney chair and an iconic Vico Magistretti sofa all communing in happy harmony. Tobias is a dab hand at this sort of thing, for he is the man behind 8 Holland Street, the London- and Bath-based gallery and design store that has become known, since launching five years ago, for its covetable offering of twentieth-century art and design. Both his cottage and the galleries are all about the mix. 'It's about juxtaposing different styles and putting pieces together in a way that pleases the eye,' explains Tobias.

There is a whiff of Kettle's Yard – the intimate modernist home of the late Jim and Helen Ede, in Cambridge – about the cottage. It's a reference that isn't lost on Tobias: as a history of art student at Cambridge, he spent a good chunk of his undergraduate days there, admiring its lived-in beauty, and the way that masterpieces and found objects were combined with such ease. Both his cottage and Kettle's Yard have white walls, but the influence of the Cambridge institution is particularly apparent in the way Tobias arranges pieces. There may not be a swirl of 76 round pebbles like at Kettle's Yard, but art, furniture and decorative objects are all approached as equally important – as pieces to be enjoyed and savoured. Vignettes are masterfully pulled together by Tobias, ranging from a quartet of blue and white tiles positioned just so in his bedroom to a pair of slipware vessels that sit perfectly on the high ledge at the top of the sitting room walls. 'Like in the interiors that I admire the most, I don't think that there should be a hierarchy between art and furniture,' he explains. 'I see an interior more as a display than something that can be broken down into separate components.'

Tobias started renting this cottage about eight years ago, attracted by the fact it was a 'miniscule' weekend bolthole. 'I just saw it as an empty space that I could throw all my things into,' says Tobias. While many interior designers crave a gut job, Tobias – who also runs an interior design service through 8 Holland Street – was thrilled that this presented the exact opposite of a project. 'I liked how the space here dictated what I could do,' he explains. The kitchen and bathroom were perfectly adequate, and there was, for example, only one spot the sofa could occupy and one wall the bed would fit on in the main bedroom. 'At work, we're constantly brainstorming for projects, so it felt hugely refreshing to have parameters set

In the sitting room of Tobias's rented cottage, the colour and pattern comes not from the walls, but an array of objects and paintings, including a huge trial for a screen print by Sandra Blow, which hangs above the fireplace, a painterly Moroccan rug and a Swedish tiled-top coffee table by Åke Holm.

for me,' Tobias clarifies. Coir carpets were fitted throughout and the walls were painted white. 'White really suits the space because it draws out all of the funny idiosyncrasies of the cottage, like the bread oven in the kitchen,' says Tobias. In this room, he had a hard-wearing green rubber floor laid – 'It's a bit like a garage floor and it totally lifts the room.'

While the majority of pieces came from his previous house in Bath, Tobias did source a few bits specifically for here. The dining table is his mum's old work desk, which perfectly suits the modest space available, with its green lino top picking up the floor. The brilliant four-poster bed in his bedroom is in fact his childhood bed from Habitat, which magically fits, with just millimeters to spare, and is now resplendent in a grass green paint. But very often, rugs and artwork are what provided the starting point for each of the five rooms. In the sitting room, a black-and-white oil painting by Swedish artist Bo Beskow, which Tobias bought at auction, became the bedrock for the room and now forms part of a gallery-style wall with other pieces from his collection. 'I get a bit scared of that kind of hang, but I just took a hammer to the wall and did the whole thing quickly,' he recalls. In fact, he reckons everything hanging in the house was likely the result of a three-hour exercise on a frustrated Saturday morning. 'I'm quite an impatient person, so I had everything up a few weeks after I'd moved in.'

The way Tobias describes building up rooms is a little like weighing out the ingredients of a recipe. And so, in the sitting room, with the gallery wall installed, he then wanted something more figurative to balance it all out and discovered a Swedish tiled-top coffee table that did just that. Then followed the rest: a painterly Moroccan rug, the 'Maralunga' sofa by Vico Magistretti, and a huge trial for a screen print by the artist Sandra Blow that Tobias bought rolled up from her studio during a sale. 'Putting together the cottage was a bit like Tetris and there isn't a single thing here that I won't want to live with wherever I am in the world,' he explains. 'I love how the orange warms the room,' he adds, referring to the Blow print. Whether this splash of colour informed the kitchen cabinets, he cannot

be sure, but he had them painted in an uncannily similar hue – Farrow & Ball's 'Dutch Orange'. Amazingly, just like the units and worktops, the tiles were already there, so Tobias left them and amped up their slightly continental holiday feel with a bunch of ceramic bananas that he picked up from a Somerset market.

Another local-market find was the painted tiled frieze that now sits above the fireplace in the kitchen, depicting a rather strange scene of people squashing grapes with their feet. 'It's medieval meets the 1960s,' says Tobias of the frieze. 'It is one of my favourite-ever finds, and I love how it's quite tongue-in-cheek and weird,' he adds. 'I want the things in my house to make me smile. Some bits are collectable and some really aren't; some were bargains and some not so much, but I love how the cottage gave me a space for my own collections aside from work.' While he has tried to keep his home quite separate from the gallery, he could not help but hang a 1965 poster for a Le Corbusier exhibition at 8 Holland Street W8 above his sofa. 'I've got one in the gallery and one here,' he says, with a smile. 'I was amazed when I found them.'

As much as Tobias is interested in the interior as a whole, he is quick to point out how individual pieces have a huge impact on each room. The 1950s Orkney chair, for instance, was once in the kitchen, but has now settled in the sitting room and feels fittingly rustic for the space. Equally, the Vico Magistretti chair in the other corner gives the room a dash of glamour. 'I used to have a 1950s oak and rope armchair by Paolo Buffa there, but the olive-green seat on the Magistretti just totally lifted the room,' he explains. Green proved equally transformative in the bathroom, where he used it as a tideline halfway up the walls. 'I got a bit bored midway through, but it does give the room a new energy,' he says. He admits to being a little embarrassed at the collection of decorative objects on the shelves in this room. 'They're all bits I collected as a teenager and I can't quite bear to get rid of them,' he explains. And so he shouldn't. For this is a home layered with a collector's eye, where so much of the joy comes through the contrast and the mix.

A vintage Vico Magistretti chair enlivens
one corner of the sitting room, behind which
is a gallery-style wall that features works
including a black and white oil painting by
Swedish artist Bo Beskow. Vico Magistretti's
'Maralunga' sofa fills the other wall perfectly,
sitting below prints and a poster for a 1965
Le Corbusier exhibition that happened
to be held at 8 Holland Street.

Inexpensive green rubber flooring from Polymax – 'the sort you'd find in an industrial garage', Tobias adds – lines the kitchen and dining room floor, picking up the colour on the top of the dining table, which was Tobias' mother's old work desk. The existing kitchen remained, but Tobias had the units repainted in Farrow & Ball's 'Dutch Orange'.

Tobias repainted his childhood Habitat four-poster bed in Farrow & Ball's 'Emerald Green', pairing it with a vintage boucherouite rug and a patchwork quilt that he bought in Delhi. The brass wall sconce is from Svenskt Tenn. The bathroom remained as Tobias found it, but he painted the bottom half of the walls with the green paint leftover from the bed.

SARAH CORBETT-WINDER

Fashion stylist and designer, north London

If you happen to be one of Sarah Corbett-Winder's 180,000-plus Instagram followers, you will know that the fashion stylist-turned-designer has a cracking sense of humour, documenting her imaginative wardrobe in locations that range from the frozen-food aisle in the supermarket to her local fish and chip shop.

Unsurprisingly, the 1930s house in north-west London, which she shares with her husband Ned (founder of Not-Another-Bill) and their three children, is every inch as playful. There are jewel-toned door frames, stripes in almost any colour you could imagine running riot over walls and furniture, and intriguing details at every turn, ranging from a chunky tiled green fireplace to a pair of classically inspired glossy dressers in the Crittall-doored kitchen that feel like something out of an English country house. 'We wanted to create our own world, which was fun and a bit crazy, but also based on tradition. Our old flat looked a bit like a Pinterest board, so we tried really hard to avoid trends here,' explains Sarah who recently founded Kipper, a brand that aims to empower women through its classically tailored suit designs. 'Like with my suits, we wanted to create something timeless that we wouldn't get bored of.'

Sarah and Ned bought the three-floor house in 2019, lured in by its brilliant lateral space and generous proportions. So ensued six months of renovating: a vast kitchen and dining area was created on the ground floor by removing a conservatory and extending by a further 3 metres, while the top floor became a suite for the couple, with a large pitched-roofed bedroom, ensuite bathroom and all-important dressing room for Sarah's burgeoning wardrobe. Doors were pushed as high as possible and little fun pediment hats were added (echoing the shape of the dressers), while chunky cornices were put in to create a sense of playful grandeur. 'It was all about opening it up,' Sarah recalls.

These architectural changes certainly shape the space, but it is colour that really anchors the interior. 'On the whole, we've themed rooms by colour,' Sarah explains. There is the study, sandwiched between the sitting room and kitchen on the ground floor, in Little Greene's warm 'Mortlake Yellow'; the red family bathroom; their eldest daughter's bedroom pretty in pink; and the blue-and-white striped office-cum-playroom on the first floor. 'It just made sense to do each room based around a colour, as it helps create a sense of flow and stops it becoming repetitive,' says Sarah. Some rooms, such as the sitting room – with its tobacco-toned walls, green tiled fireplace and eclectic mix of furniture – do not adhere quite so strictly to one particular colour, but they are still conceived around the belief that the relationship between colours is vital. 'Everything has to come from the same family,' Sarah insists.

174

A dresser painted in 'Brinjal' by Farrow & Ball complements raw plaster walls and a pink polished concrete floor. An Arlo & Jacob armchair and a 'Citron Glazed Vase with Lemon Decoration' from Shropshire Design add a punchy pop.

'In the same way that I put an outfit together, I've tried to keep the house tonal and earthy, with the occasional pop rather than having too many crazy colours,' she explains. There is a good amount of brown weaving its way throughout the space, cropping up on the lower portion of the hallway walls and on the stair runner. 'Ned was worried it might be a bit ugly, but it just really grounds the house,' says Sarah. 'We wanted the house to provide a calm backdrop to family life.'

A case in point is the kitchen, where the raw plaster walls, pink polished concrete floor and white units are enlivened by an aubergine dresser, a mustard armchair, and a wall stacked high with art and plates. 'They're all pieces we've collected over the years,' explains Sarah. 'Some are by our children and others are by Ned's mother, Kate Corbett Winder, who is an artist.' An unexpected vibrant pop comes in from a wonderful multi-coloured corduroy striped seat cushion that runs the entire length – plus a bit more – of the 4-metre-long kitchen table, atop a built-in olive green banquette. 'We actually had the bench cushion made after we'd lived here for about three years,' explains Sarah. 'Initially, we'd gone for a mustard yellow, but the room could take something stronger and we've become a bit braver in our choices after a few years here.' For a similar reason, the ottoman in the sitting room has taken on a new guise in a bright green corduroy, while their own bedroom – once all white walls – has become an orange and white affair in 'Tented Stripe' wallpaper from Farrow & Ball. 'We would never have dreamt of doing that when we moved in, but the stripe makes it so cosy,' explains Sarah.

Stripes, in fact, are one of the few patterns that she has really embraced in the house. 'I appreciate patterns in other people's houses, but I really struggled to find a way to make it work here,' explains Sarah, who only ventured into the world of florals in her eldest daughter's room, with curtains made from 'Dahlia Red' by Sarah Vanrenan at The Fabric Collective. 'I feel that the stripe will be here forever, whereas I was conscious

of choosing a pattern and then seeing it everywhere and going off it,' she adds. In the family bathroom, she flipped a red-and-white striped wallpaper from Ralph Lauren so that it now runs horizontally around the room, teaming it with a blind in Ian Mankin's 'Devon Stripe' and diagonally striped floor tiles from London Encaustic. Her eldest and youngest children's adjoining bedrooms are something of a stripe-fest too, with mustard-and-white striped walls and ceiling – Ferm Living's 'Thick Lines' wallpaper – leading onto green striped walls. It is a clever decorating choice for a children's room, which will hopefully provide a lasting backdrop as they grow up.

A room, however, that has seen some change is a former guest bedroom: the wardrobes were moved to create a partition, providing an ad-hoc play space for the children and a defined studio for Sarah. 'It was the blue room, as we'd painted the walls in a bluey-green colour called "Livid" from Little Greene,' Sarah recalls. 'But I could just never connect with it as a block of colour, which is quite funny, considering its name,' she says, with a laugh. And so, when Sarah decided to convert the space into her office for Kipper, she thought it was time to create a rather more inspiring backdrop, turning to London-based artist Lucy Mahon to add something she knew would work: hand-painted blue and white stripes. 'They've just totally transformed the room,' says Sarah. 'While we don't plan on redecorating on a massive scale, it's nice to return to rooms and think about how you could do them a bit differently.'

Aside from colour, this is an interior defined by stuff – or what Sarah refers to as 'organised clutter'. China dogs, ceramic fruit, plates, botanical prints, wooden boats – this is a home crammed full of the rich layers of family life, where things mean something and conjure up memories of holidays and special times. Ultimately, it is a house conceived around the idea of joy and it succeeds in doing the most important thing of all – it makes you smile.

Painted in Paint & Paper Library's 'Caddie',
the sitting room features a fireplace made from
tiles from London Encaustic and an Arlo & Jacob
ottoman upholstered in a bright green corduroy.
In the next door study, the walls and shelves
are painted in Little Greene's 'Mortlake Yellow',
which provides a backdrop to a sofa that Sarah
created in collaboration with Birdie Fortescue
and a Tate & Darby rug.

In Sarah's studio, the hand-painted blue-and-white striped walls are by London-based artist Lucy Mahon. Sarah's daughter's bedroom is one of the few rooms in the house to feature a floral, with curtains made from 'Dahlia Red' by Sarah Vanrenan at The Fabric Collective. The quilt is by Projektityyny.

The bathroom is half-papered in 'Mapleton Stripe' by Ralph Lauren with a blind in Ian Mankin's 'Devon Stripe' cotton in peony. The main bedroom ceiling was opened up to reveal a pitched roof and is papered from top-to-toe in Farrow & Ball's 'Tented Stripe' wallpaper. The quilt is from Toast.

GAVIN HOUGHTON

Interior designer, ceramicist and artist, south London

'If I have an idea, I jump,' says Gavin Houghton. It figures, for he somehow balances a successful interior design business with making his highly sought-after ceramics and hosting sketching holidays in Tangier with his good friend and former *World of Interiors* art director Joan Hecktermann. 'I don't like sitting around,' he adds, mentioning a couple of his current ideas that include a collection of wallpapers (imminent) and the decoration of a doll's house (still in the dreaming stage). 'The more you do, the more you want to do,' explains Gavin, who trained in menswear before landing a job at *World of Interiors* and then moving into interior design in 2008.

Rather like its owner, his house – a joyfully decorated, colourful Victorian terrace in Stockwell – is not the sort that sits still. Paintings come and go, rooms take on new purposes, and beloved bits and bobs move around. 'I recently hung that painting,' he says, gesturing to an impressionistic portrait of a man, which sits above the fireplace in the sitting room. 'There used to be a mirror there, but I sold it to a client, and then I found this picture on Instagram, which feels perfect.' Crucially, Gavin's changes have never been about moving walls or even, on the whole, altering anything as significant as curtains. In fact, wallpapers and colours rarely change, instead providing the framework for an ever-evolving cast of decorative objects and pictures.

Gavin moved to the four-floor house 20 years ago, attracted by the fact it was a 'charming shambles' that had not been done up. At this point, he was just starting to think about doing interiors for other people, and this house became a laboratory where he could test ideas and refine his style, which offers a playful take on traditional English decoration. 'I guess my aesthetic is a nod to Charleston, with a splash of David Hicks and John Fowler,' says Gavin. 'I like bright and loud, but I'm not a fan of dirge.' His house is testament to that, with pattern-on-pattern, strong colours and a hint of theatre.

'The bay window in the sitting room kick-started a whole thing for me, as you couldn't have a curtain pole, so I got into pelmets,' explains Gavin. 'I don't really like the urban aesthetic, and this set the scene for quite a country, chintzy look.' The house certainly feels more of the countryside than the city, layered up with florals, deep sofas and art. There is a fireplace in almost every room: an impressive marble one, lined with Delft tiles from Douglas Watson, in Gavin's bedroom and an ornate carved wooden one in the dining room that he bought from a sale at Sibyl Colefax & John Fowler before they moved from Brook Street in Mayfair. 'I bought it after a drunk lunch, when I was feeling rather rich,' he admits, laughing. Another carved wooden fireplace, picked up for significantly less on Golborne Road, takes centre stage in the sitting room. 'It's far too grand for my house, but I love it,' he says.

Gavin Houghton's sitting room is painted in a dark cosseting green – Dulux Trade's '90YY 13/177' – which is offset by a honey-coloured ceiling. The carved wooden fireplace – 'far too grand for my house', jokes Gavin – came from a shop on Golborne Road, while the impressionistic portrait above came from Instagram.

Greens snake their way throughout the house and amp up the country feel. Downstairs, Pierre Frey's naturalistic 'Espalier' wallpaper provides a backdrop to the dining area, along with an old green dresser that plays host to ceramics and glassware. The paper is typical of Gavin's aesthetic – grounded in tradition, but fresh and joyful. 'I'm a bit stuck in a groove when it comes to using green, but I love that there is such a spectrum of tones within it,' he says, gesturing to the cosseting dark green walls of the sitting room, which he has tempered with a rich honey-coloured ceiling. 'It's like the colour you'd find in a smokey pub,' Gavin says. Elsewhere, wallpapers run riot: from a rich green floral hand-painted de Gournay wallpaper in the hall to a Bloomsbury-esque foliage- and diamond-adorned pattern in his bedroom. 'That's just the most perfect design and scale,' says Gavin of the print by Brunschwig & Fils. 'I'm quite addicted to wallpaper, especially when they get the balance and repeat just right,' he adds. 'I guess I've always been intrigued by surface design.'

For a man who loves repeats, he is equally embracing of imperfections. 'I like dog-eared,' he says, grinning. Nothing is quite in that state, but this is a house where scuffs are tolerated and where nothing is laboured or taken too seriously. Objects find their spot but there is no meticulous scheming, and he buys things for their beauty rather than as part of a plan. 'I've ended up with a collection of miniatures on this fireplace, but it wasn't something that I planned,' says Gavin, pointing out a selection of pieces that include a plaster leaf by artist Viola Lanari, an African figurine and a blue ceramic camel. 'I don't really ever buy things from posh shops. They're just things that I find when I'm travelling, or buy from artists and

makers,' he explains. 'I really don't like over-thought-out rooms. Something has to be slightly off.'

This attitude also informs his approach to ceramics, which he has been making in the red shed at the bottom of his garden since the 2020 lockdown. 'Rather than perfect wheel-thrown pots, everything I make is slab-built,' he says of his charming, often cheekily decorated, plates, vases and tiles. Many of his rejects or trials are dotted around the house, along with other ceramics that he has collected over the years, including Delft plates that he inherited from his uncle, which now hang on the walls. 'As a student, I used to use them for dinner parties,' he recalls. 'I didn't know what they were back then.' For Gavin, the joy of making ceramics is in the process: 'You get a bag of clay and after a bit of effort you end up with a beautiful thing, which is so satisfying,' he says. His approach to decorating has always been similarly hands-on. There is a sewing machine hidden underneath the dining table, with which he has whipped up his fair share of curtains and cushions, having learned how to sew as a fashion student.

Art plays a big part in the house, and ranges from Duncan Grants to pieces by artists that Gavin has discovered on Instagram. 'I like painterly, decorative, sketchy stuff,' explains Gavin, who also enjoys painting. 'I am a bit of an addict when it comes to buying pictures and I'm always moving them around.' Like with his ceramics, the joy of decorating comes from the process – of changing things up, experimenting and not being too precious. It also comes from the belief that houses should be ever-evolving. 'It's a place in constant happy flux,' Gavin concludes.

Howe's 'Den' sofa runs along the sitting room wall, with a sketch by artist Duncan Grant amongst the pieces hanging above. The hallway is papered in a dusky green floral wallpaper from de Gournay, which provides a backdrop to an oil painting by Gavin of a man in Tangier and a sketch by artist Luke Edward Hall (see his house on pages 78–89).

In the basement kitchen and dining room, the walls are papered in 'Espalier' by Pierre Frey, while the fireplace came from a sale at Sibyl Colefax & John Fowler before they moved from Brook Street in Mayfair. The antique green painted dresser came from a junk shop in Chipping Norton.

Gavin's bedroom is papered in 'Gallier
Diamond' by Brunschwig & Fils – an all-
time favourite pattern of his. The cushions
on the bed are made up from a fabric by
Madeleine Castaing, while the ornate marble
chimneypiece, lined with tiles made by
Douglas Watson, was a leftover from a job.
The painting above is from one of Gavin's
favourite junk shops in Chipping Norton.

The ground floor bathroom is papered
in 'Richmond Park' by Zoffany, while the
upstairs bathroom is two-tone. The red
shed at the bottom of Gavin's garden is
both his interior design and ceramics studio,
with a small kiln outside to fire his creations.

FEE GREENING

Illustrator, Dorset

Illustrator Fee Greening's seventeenth-century thatched cottage looks like it could have sprung from one of her whimsical dip pen and ink drawings. There are its glossy yellow window frames and its location, deep in the Dorset countryside, next to a copse of poplars and a stream where Patti, her blue merle border collie, happily frolics. And then there is the earthy palette inside, which provides a backdrop to many of the motifs in Fee's creations – from butterflies clustered in frames to sea monsters carved into the back of a pair of chairs. In the garden, Fee's shepherd's hut studio – nicknamed 'Baba Yaga' by the artist after a Slavic folklore witch – is equally otherworldly, with a floral-fabric-laden bed and walls pinned with Fee's drawings. 'It's the first time since I was a child that I've ever had a space completely of my own,' she says, of the hut. 'It's my own little world and makes me feel so much more confident as an artist,' adds Fee, whose clients include Gucci, Florence + the Machine and wallpaper brand CommonRoom.

Fee and her boyfriend, record producer and guitarist Dan White, bought the cottage in early 2022. They had left London for Dorset two years before, mid-pandemic and on a bit of a whim, and had been renting a ramshackle cottage in the grounds of Lulworth Castle. 'Two months became two years, and we couldn't imagine moving back to London, so

we decided to hunt for our own place,' explains Fee, who grew up in Devon and had always planned to move back to the west country. They trawled satellite maps looking for a little cottage set on its own that might be in their budget, and sent out handwritten letters to the owners, enquiring if they might perhaps be looking to sell. 'Neighbours aren't really ideal when Dan's recording guitars,' Fee explains. By curious coincidence, this cottage appeared on Rightmove just as the couple were driving there to deliver their note. 'We went straight there,' recalls Fee. 'I burst into tears the moment we walked in and Dan couldn't look directly at it, because he just loved it so much,' she adds, laughing. Thankfully, their offer was accepted. 'We'd been looking at places without roofs, but we were lucky here, as we inherited a half-done project,' Fee says. 'The previous owners had done all the really brutal bits, like replacing the thatch and rewiring.'

Although it still needed a fair bit of work – and will for a while, including new bathrooms – the couple decided to start by painting the cottage in warm, happy colours. 'It might seem a strange thing to do, but for us it made sense to create somewhere that felt jolly and homely while we saved up for bigger works,' explains Fee, who got to work on the painting with Dan and a few willing friends – fortuitously, a decorator and a decorative painter – the moment they got

Fee Greening's utility room features
a door curtain made from Morris &
Co fabric, which Fee's mum stitched
up for her. The little letter rack was,
like many of the things in Fee's
house, a lucky eBay find.

the keys. The window frames – outside and in – were the first to receive an update and are painted in a glossy egg-yolk yellow inspired by a room of the same colour in The Square & Compass pub in nearby Worth Matravers. 'It's one of our favourite places in the world, so it's our ode to that,' explains Fee. Yellow continues inside too: one bedroom – the couple, in fact, move between the two upstairs bedrooms as the mood takes them – is limewashed in a more muted butterscotch, while there are curtains throughout made by Fee's mum out of yellow Morris & Co patterns. She also whipped up what Fee refers to as 'headbangers' – the fabric-wrapped foam pads hanging above the doors. 'Someone hit their head straight away and it was just miserable, so this was our solution,' Fee explains. 'But it was also quite a good way to bring in an extra layer of colour and homeliness.'

Rather than being the result of schemes and moodboards, this is an interior that has grown out of the rich, earthy colours that the couple love, use in their work or wear – dark olives, chocolates, rusty oranges and ochres. 'The house is basically the same colour as the socks we wear,' says Fee, with a grin. 'And a lot of the colour comes from pieces that we've collected together since we were students,' she adds, pointing out the frames of butterflies above their bed, which she bought when the couple were first living together in a shared house. 'They were damaged, so we spent a couple of evenings watching films and re-pinning them,' recalls Fee. 'The colours of everything we like is in those butterflies.'

This includes the burnt orange on the walls in the sitting room, which is a shade that also often appears in Fee's work. 'I wanted to embrace the fact that this was a dark room, and the orange on the walls amps up the drama and feels like fiery dragon embers,' she explains. The idea to pair them with a blue cupboard came about when Fee was painting the walls and realised how good her jeans looked alongside the orange. 'It's all about getting the balance between colours right and this combination looked cool, so I decided to search on eBay for a blue cupboard,' Fee explains. Thankfully, it delivered. 'We're eBay fiends,' she adds, gesturing to a lime green Anglepoise lamp and a pair of carved wooden chairs she found on there. 'I've got alerts set up for anything to do with demons, serpents or sea monsters,' she confides, explaining how she stumbled upon one of her other favourite purchases – a £10 pair of metal candlesticks in the site's Halloween section.

Of all the rooms, the kitchen is perhaps the one that brings together all the colours the couple love, with its cheerful yellow cabinets, a dark olive sideboard, tiles featuring Fee's drawings of wild flowers and serpents that she created in collaboration with bathroom brand Balineum, and a Zardi & Zardi tapestry. 'I got it for an absolute steal at a sample sale and it has followed us around forever,' explains Fee. 'It's a big inspiration for my work, but Dan also loves it because it soaks up sound.' It also features Fee's beloved heathery pink: 'I guess my palette is quite medieval,' Fee suggests. This influence also extends to the shepherd's hut, where cut-out arches framing the built-in bed are based on the kind found in illuminated manuscripts. 'They often put the action of the story within a frame, so it's my take on that,' says Fee, who decked out the bed in 'Floralia', a pretty design from Schumacher's Cabana collection. Walls painted in 'Churlish Green' and red woodwork in 'Bamboozle', both by Farrow & Ball, continue the medieval reference.

Throughout, the couple's inspirations are wonderfully original and offbeat. The slime green ceiling in the sweet utility room, for instance, takes its cue from the colour that Dan has currently chosen to dye his hair, while upstairs the butterscotch bedroom is Fee's take on *Little Women* meets *Calamity Jane*. 'I guess there is something a bit cowboy about it,' says Fee with a grin, gesturing to the rusty-red woodwork and unusual window drapes made from a Voysey fabric featuring castles and hounds. At the other end of the house, the larger bedroom takes its lead from the nursery in the 1991 film *Hook*, with walls in a soft apricot-goldy colour. 'It's such a core memory for me,' says Fee. 'And this room just reminded me of it, with its sloping ceilings, so I wanted to do something quite elegant and dreamy.' In here, the curtains, while no less pirate ship-esque, are made from Bennison's 'Chinese Toile', a romantic gauzy patterned linen.

Just as the palette is grounded in the earthy colours of the natural world, so are many of the things within the cottage. Stacks of sticks and driftwood, foraged on walks, are propped up against walls, while hag stones – those with a naturally occurring hole that are said to have talismanic qualities – and shells adorn the surfaces. 'I am most relaxed when I'm in the thick of nature, and I pick things up that feel good and end up bringing them back,' explains Fee. 'I almost feel like they cast a protective spell on the house.' Whether you believe in such magic or not, one thing is for sure: Fee has certainly cast her spell here.

The couple's love of the colour yellow is
reflected in both the window frames and
kitchen units, which are painted yellow,
colour-matched to a piece of paper that
Fee had. A Zardi & Zardi tapestry, bought
for a steal from a sample sale, features
many of Fee's favourite, medieval-inspired
colours. The tiles behind the sink are
from Fee's collaboration with Balineum.

Walls in 'Carrot' by Bauwerk give warmth
to the sitting room. The blue cupboard
was an eBay find, inspired when Fee was
painting the room and realised how good
her blue jeans looked alongside the paint.
Fabric wrapped 'headbangers' were Fee's
solution to stopping people from banging
their heads, providing a vehicle for more
colour and pattern.

Limewashed butterscotch walls create
a cocooning feel in one of the two bedrooms.
The butterfly specimens came from eBay,
but were damaged so Fee spent a few evenings
meticulously repinning them. In the other
bedroom, unusual window drapes are made
from Bennison's 'Chinese Toile' in charcoal
on beige. The hallway is densely hung with
prints and posters the couple have collected.

Fee's shepherd's hut is painted in 'Churlish Green', with woodwork in 'Bamboozle' – both by Farrow & Ball. The built-in bedframe is painted in Annie Sloan's 'Olive' chalk paint and the bed is covered in Schumacher's 'Floralia', with cushions in their 'Annika Floral Tapestry' and also in Fee's own 'Pearl Twist' fabric in olive. The yellow glossy window frames are painted in an outdoor paint from B&Q, colour-matched to a piece of paper that Fee had.

JAMES MACKIE

Designer, Oxfordshire

'I'm drawn to quite an earthy palette,' says James Mackie, former Sotheby's specialist turned interior designer, when I ask about his approach to decoration. 'Browns, oranges, greens, blues and dashes of yellow mixed with neutrals – for me they're the most natural colours in the world,' he adds, explaining that he has gravitated to the same tones since he was a teenager, when he would pore over books by renowned decorator and colourist David Hicks. 'My love for these colours came partly from his work and partly from growing up in the countryside in Devon,' says James.

After an interlude of a couple of decades in London, James is back in the countryside, in a mellow-stoned seventeenth-century former labourer's cottage in Oxfordshire. An homage to his favourite colours, the space is small – just two bedrooms – but it is rich and layered, with a good spattering of art, particularly prints, and a thoughtfully chosen selection of furniture. The interiors have developed alongside James's own evolution. When he bought it in 2016, he was still heading up the Impressionist and Modern Art department at Sotheby's, in London, and the cottage was a weekend bolthole. But in 2020, he left his job, moved full-time to the countryside and, buoyed by his experience of renovating the cottage, launched interior design studio J. James Mackie, which *House & Garden* named as one of the Top 100 interior design studios in 2023. 'I guess the cottage is the most powerful representation of what I'd do when left completely to my own devices,' says James, grinning. 'It's me let loose as a decorator.'

And let loose he has – to brilliant effect. 'I wanted to make a virtue of the fact it was a series of small rooms and create a rich jewel box,' recalls James, who spent nine months overhauling the cottage in 2019, and plenty more days since, tweaking. There were some pretty major changes: a sad lean-to was replaced with an elegant Arts and Crafts-inspired panelled extension that now houses James's collection of art books; a former junk room became a charming guest bedroom that is now papered top-to-toe in Morris & Co's 'Willow Bough'; and a warren of small rooms downstairs became a space that is as joyful as it is useful, with a shower and laundry room, and an arsenic-coloured built-in bar. 'Decorating is all about balance and harmony,' says James, who is a dab hand when it comes to mixing bolder flourishes with calmer elements. Joyful apple-green kitchen units, for instance, are balanced with white walls and a simple sawn-oak table, while the 'Willow Bough' walls of the spare bedroom are tempered by the plain orange quilt on the bed.

Although James loves colour and pattern, he stresses that it has to be 'marshalled'. A good case in point is his bedroom, where the pattern – introduced through the Lewis & Wood

What was a warren of small rooms downstairs became a series of jewel boxes: the bathroom, painted in Farrow & Ball's 'India Yellow', leads onto a tiny bar area that is painted in Farrow & Ball's 'Arsenic' with a curtain underneath made from Bennison's 'Woodcut' linen.

border running around the top of the room, the colourful bedcover and the curtains in Sibyl Colefax & John Fowler's 'Strawberry Leaf' – has been balanced out by walls in 'Oval Room Blue' by Farrow & Ball. 'You need to know where to push and pull, because you want a space to have a dynamism, but you don't want it to feel cacophonous,' he explains. Another point James is strict on, no doubt informed by the fact he studied architectural history at university, is that the building itself must dictate the decoration. 'I spent a lot of time thinking about the fact this was a labourer's cottage and I wanted to remain true to the humble nature of the place,' explains James. As such, for every bit of velvet or rich decorative detailing, there is seagrass flooring and muddy-toned woodwork. Upstairs, in the bathroom – a room, James says, that 'makes my heart sing a bit' – a pretty red-and-white wallpaper from Howe and an ornate gilt mirror are grounded by woodwork painted in a chocolate brown from Farrow & Ball. Similarly, in the sitting room, a jaunty oversized scagliola column feels less Grand Tour, thanks to the simple seagrass squares underfoot.

The sitting room and the book-room extension that it leads onto have recently been the subject of a rethink. 'At first I conceived of these rooms as quite separate, but after living with them for a few years, I realised I wanted to make them more cohesive,' says James, explaining that the book room is the only space in the house with real volume and proper ceiling height. In the sitting room, white walls were painted in a lively orange by Edward Bulmer – 'Malahide' – turning the space into a cosy den, which is ideal in the winter months. 'I then decided it was time to get rid of the painfully uncomfortable eighteenth-century box sofa and went for a classic squidgy country-house sofa, which is much more fit for purpose,' says James, laughing. Next, he brought a Persian rug from upstairs down to the book room, which tonally links the space to the sitting room and dictated a new palette. Accordingly, a Howard & Sons armchair was reupholstered in a beloved blue-and-orange Bennison fabric that James had bought years before from a sale, while the sofa in here was re-covered in a rich green velvet. 'That's the way I like to decorate: with a bit of print, a bit of velvet and a bit of rush matting,' explains James.

He is endlessly tinkering with rooms, but he admits that he did properly scheme for these two rooms. 'I was pretty methodical in how I approached it, as there were basically six elements that were going to change, and each impacted the next,' he explains. He confesses that for each room he often has five or so schemes in his head. 'There is always another way of doing a room that would be just as beautiful,' he says. Often, however, he will simply add a new piece of furniture or artwork and see what it does. Equally, he is clear that art should not have the upper hand in a room. 'I buy and sell lots of art, often upgrading to better pieces when I can, but I try not to let them dominate,' explains James, whose print collection includes work by artists such as David Hockney and Graham Sutherland. 'It's fun to mess about with rooms and just see what works,' he adds. 'That's the joy of decorating.'

In the kitchen and dining area, the units
are painted in Farrow & Ball's 'Sap Green', while
the limestone floor was already there. A sawn-
oak Arts and Crafts dining table and eighteenth
century chairs, sourced from RN Myers & Son
add to the cottage feel. Just glimpsed is a small
staircase, papered in Morris & Co's 'Willow
Bough', which leads up to the guest bedroom
that is in the same paper.

Walls in Edward Bulmer's 'Malahide' give
a warmth to the sitting room, along with the
seagrass matting underfoot, which came
from eBay. The book room, which occupies
the extension that James added and features
a deep bay window and ceilings so high
that James needn't stoop, is painted in
Edward Bulmer's 'Mummy'. The armchair
is in Bennison's now discontinued 'Tapestry'.

James's bedroom is painted in Farrow & Ball's 'Oval Room Blue', with Lewis & Wood's 'Bacchus' border running around the top and curtains in Sibyl Colefax & John Fowler's 'Strawberry Leaf'. The bathroom is papered in Howe at 36 Bourne Street's 'Knurl' in brick, with woodwork in 'Salon Drab' by Farrow & Ball in gloss.

PETER THWAITES & REBECCA AIRD

Fabric designers and printers, Gloucestershire

Peter Thwaites and Rebecca Aird are at the helm of Rapture & Wright, one of the few companies in England to design and hand-print its wallpapers and fabrics sustainably in-house. Or, to be more specific, conjure them up from a 15-metre long printing table in a low-impact workshop in Gloucestershire that has its own off-grid living water drainage system. 'Our goal is to be completely self-sufficient by 2030,' Rebecca says, telling me that they have recently clad the roof of the barn in solar panels. Rebecca and Peter, a husband and wife with previous careers in graphic design and set building, respectively, launched the company in 2004, and moved to the current premises – a previously redundant cow barn – on Rebecca's family farm in 2017.

The story of their house is intrinsically linked to what they do, for not only is it brimful of their own joyful creations, but it also occupies the barn next to their workshop. It is the closest we come to a new build with this book, though technically it is the conversion of an old Dutch barn and sheep dip. All that was salvageable was the skeletal steel structure, which Rebecca and Peter then patched in with insulated panels and humble materials that would serve as a reminder of the building's agricultural past – charred ash cladding and a galvanised steel corrugated roof. What that created inside was a clean-lined, flexible space. The main barrel-roofed part consists of two floors, with a single-storey wing at either end:

one accommodating more bedrooms, and the other a large room that plays host to photo shoots, yoga and just about everything else. 'Wing sounds rather grand,' says Peter, with a chuckle. 'They were formerly lean-tos, and we just matched their footprint.'

Rather like the prints they are known for – where, say, florals are enlarged and abstracted, and Delft tiles are recoloured – Peter and Rebecca wanted to create a country house that offered a fresh take on tradition. 'We didn't want it to be pastiche, but we also didn't want it to feel screamingly contemporary,' Peter explains. How did the clean lines of the space inform their approach to the decoration? 'It liberated us enormously,' Peter immediately says. 'We used to live in a low-ceilinged seventeenth-century chocolate-box Cotswolds cottage and, lovely as it was, it was incredibly inflexible.' Here the couple had the freedom to create something special, which could also work as a showcase for their work. Of course, in many ways, their own fabrics and wallpapers, which are used almost exclusively throughout the house – with the exception of a couple of plains – set the palette, which is a mix of greens, blues and browns, with stronger highlights elsewhere.

The large open-plan living area is the *pièce de résistance*, running the length of the main part of the building downstairs, with the kitchen at one end, the dining table in the middle and a large sitting area at the other end. A big determining

factor in their decoration of this space was the view of the landscape, which is something of a focal point thanks to a wall of floor-to-ceiling doors. 'We didn't want anything inside to be overly distracting,' explains Rebecca. The living space, with its washed-wood matchboard walls, is all muddy browns and greens. Curtains are made from the company's 'Tabriz' fabric, inspired by an ottoman tile design; a pair of armchairs are in 'Kuba', an abstract design inspired by both seventeenth-century African Kuba cloth and 1950s woodcuts; and the sofa is in 'Delft', a playful floral inspired by a seventeenth-century tile. The deep purple and white rug underfoot was created in collaboration with rug designer Amy Kent: it is an enlarged version of their 'Albaicin' design, inspired by a work by British land artist and sculptor Richard Long. 'These four patterns have totally different influences that span hundreds of years, but they work so well together,' Peter says. Their 'Albaicin' design, in blue, also fills the wall, in wallpaper form, and runs from the dining area to the kitchen, while the pattern also crops up on a headboard in one of the guest rooms – a tiny but visually impressive space papered in another of their patterns. 'Doing the house has made us see our designs in a new light,' explains Peter.

While tones from the natural world shape the palette, the couple also introduced stronger and bolder dashes. There is the 1970s red lamp, which livens up a little twin bedroom that otherwise has all the ingredients of a classic country-house bedroom. Peter – who admits to being the 'flouncy person who obsesses over the details', while Rebecca focuses more on the layout – is very good when it comes to deploying these unexpected shots. In the living area, the red interlocking lacquer coffee table in the centre lifts the entire room; in the dining and kitchen area, red chairs pack a punch, as does a cheerful dresser that the couple had made bespoke.

And then there is the loo – not quite red, but a rich raspberry paint, with the top of the walls in a similarly raspberry-toned Arts and Crafts-inspired wallpaper that Rapture & Wright created in collaboration with the National Trust. 'I liked the idea that pops of red would connect each room and give the house a flow,' explains Peter.

His playful approach reigns supreme in the joyfully colourful kitchen, where a wall of cupboards resembles the sherbet version of a Mondrian painting. 'I wanted to break the cupboards up with colour, so that they didn't look like a heavy lump,' explains Peter. 'We didn't want it to feel like an obvious built-in kitchen, but wanted it to feel like a piece of furniture that worked with the rest of the house,' he explains. Other components have been accordingly tweaked, so the kitchen serves all the necessary practical functions, but feels less utilitarian. The island, which cleverly accommodates the oven, is painted olive green and has been lifted up on legs so that it 'sits a little lighter in the room', while the back row of units have been painted in an uplifting blue that is picked up by the enamel pendant lights hanging over the island.

Unsurprisingly, for a man who used to work in set design, the house is full of these unexpected flourishes. Take one of the large guest rooms, which Peter and Rebecca created in collaboration with their studio: it is papered top-to-toe in their 'Iznik' design, with large floral hand painted curtains and the bottom quarter of the walls in a *trompe l'oeil* creation whipped up by Peter. 'I guess we just needed a bit of a break from the paper,' he says with a grin. 'I love the colour combinations in here,' he adds, referring to the fact that pink, green, brown, orange and cream sit happily together. 'It's a very freeing house and has taught us a lot about how we design,' concludes Peter.

Rapture & Wright's 'Albaicin' lines one of the walls in the kitchen. The colourful units — designed to stop it feeling like a classic built-in kitchen — were made locally from ash that came from the farm. The worktops are made from slate to give it a humble feel.

A twin guest bedroom features headboards
upholstered in 'Delft' in burnt orange, while
the downstairs loo is papered in 'Webb's
Wonder' in raspberry – both from Rapture
& Wright. Another guest bedroom features
walls in the brand's 'Tin Glaze' in bronze
green, with a headboard in 'Albaicin' in palm.

CARLOS GARCIA

Interior designer, Norfolk

Interior designer Carlos Garcia is something of a poster boy for English country-house style, bringing joy to his clients and many thousands of Instagram followers alike. 'Being Spanish means that I don't have any of the inherited hang-ups about what is right or wrong for an English interior,' says the designer, who launched his eponymous one-man-band studio in 2009, and recently added a collection of beautiful fabrics and bespoke furniture to his offering. What I find interesting is that, as a European, Carlos manages to define what English decoration means today through his layered and richly detailed creations. 'Interior design shouldn't be about perfection, but it should enhance your life, and make you feel happy and comfortable,' he explains.

Nowhere does this ring truer than at his own seventeenth-century red-brick farmhouse in north Norfolk, where the decoration functions, Carlos says, 'as a pot of ideas for projects'. It is not at all what Carlos envisaged himself and his husband Michael living in – 'I'd always wanted perfectly proportioned Georgian' – but in many ways it is the Goldilocks of houses for them: neither too big or too small, nor overly grand or modest. Some rooms have panelling, good height and charming cornices, but there are also smaller proportioned spaces, such as the kitchen, which has all the charm of a cottage, with original Norfolk pamments underfoot – a happy discovery under a lino floor. While the long and low house had

been added to since it was built in 1635, the layout worked well, at mostly one-room deep, with a good flow between spaces. Downstairs, the rooms read as an enfilade, with the grander drawing room and dining room to one side of the entrance hall, and the kitchen, pantry – an enviable space that is the same size as the kitchen – and snug to the other.

Unsurprisingly for a designer who advocates decorating slowly, Carlos approached his farmhouse gently. 'We moved in, did the basics and then things started to find their natural order,' explains Carlos, who now lives in Norfolk pretty much full-time, nipping into London as and when work requires. To start with, he whipped the kitchen and their bedroom into habitable states – a clever move that allowed the rest of the house to evolve bit by bit over about five years. Gradually, fireplaces were opened up, and metres of green carpet were pulled up to reveal original wooden floors and, in the entrance hall, hexagonal tiles with 'ravishing' terracotta inserts, which were hiding under 10 cm of concrete and thick tar. The drawing room and dining room swapped places: the former took the prize spot at one end of the house, and the latter gained a cupboard, which Carlos transformed into a pink jewel-box that now plays host to his china collection.

Colour and pattern may feature prominently, but many of the walls are painted in soothing neutrals. The kitchen, painted in Edward Bulmer's jolly 'Olympian Green' to 'make you happy

in dark Norfolk winters', is an exception, but the majority of the rooms are in muddier tones. 'I like colour, but I didn't want the wall colours to take centre stage,' explains Carlos. 'Instead, I wanted to create a canvas on which everything else could be thrown,' he adds. The drawing room, painted in Farrow & Ball's 'Bone' is brought to life by Heriz rugs, a colourful suzani draped over the back of the cushion-laden sofa, and blue and white Delft pottery. In the snug, painted in Edward Bulmer's 'Milk White', the colour comes in through paintings hanging from picture rails, as well as yet more rugs, suzani cushions and gathered fabric lampshades. 'I love using colour in things that can move around,' explains Carlos. One of the guest rooms, once painted in a punchy green that Carlos admits to soon tiring of, is now painted in 'Quaker' by Edward Bulmer, which provides a backdrop to the colour that comes in through rugs, art and curtains, as well as the hangings on Carlos's own 'Gillows Bed' design, which are made from his 'Kandili' fabric. 'I absolutely love using fabrics to bring texture and pattern into a room,' says Carlos. 'This fabric, which is based on a nineteenth-century Turkish scarf, has a lot of me in it,' he says.

One other way in which Carlos likes to inject colour is by using it on the walls of areas that you pass through, such as hallways and loos. 'I like to use stronger colours in places you don't linger in, to create joyful surprises,' says Carlos, gesturing to an upstairs hallway that is painted in Edward Bulmer's 'Turquoise'. The colour is sandwiched between the pale blue walls of a guest bedroom and a soft pink bathroom, half in Edward Bulmer's 'Jonquil' and half in Robert Kime's rather pretty 'St Abbs' wallpaper. 'They're all based on the same pigments, and the blue and pink are heightened by the turquoise in the hall,' explains Carlos. 'Decorating is a bit like a symphony – there are moments of quiet, moments of surprise and moments of pure joy. I wanted the house to feel like a bit of a journey.'

Adding to this sense of journey is the way in which Carlos has mixed furniture, art and textiles to create the feeling of a home that has developed over many years. 'It wasn't about creating a set piece, but rather building layers to create the sense of a home that has been here for almost 500 years,' he explains. Where the architecture is a little muddled – the main bedroom alone has seventeenth-century doors, eighteenth-century panelling and a Victorian chimneypiece – Carlos has used this as a tool to inspire the decoration. Therefore, some pieces nod to the house's seventeenth-century origins, such as the magnificent oak court cupboard in the dining room and the seventeenth-century verdure tapestry behind it. Others, such as the Gillows bedposts in the main bedroom and the ornate gilt mirror in the drawing room, pay homage to the eighteenth century. And then there are the pieces that really represent Carlos – Spanish pottery from his grandmother, suzanis and, of course, his own fabrics. 'It's about weaving these things together,' he explains. 'What ties it all together is that everything means something to me or Michael, regardless of what period it is from.'

In the kitchen, Carlos – who admits an enduring dislike for fitted kitchens – has paired hand-built units by a local carpenter with freestanding dressers, a painted dining table and a mishmash of old country chairs that give the sense they have been gathered by successive generations. 'I didn't want everything to be the same,' explains Carlos. The two dressers make his point manifest: one is Welsh and very early – 'The sort that could have been here from the very beginning,' Carlos suggests – and one is likely from the 1950s, which Carlos found in a vintage shop in nearby Holt. 'One thing I thought a great deal about is the fact that there would have been people living here in the 1950s in a way that felt appropriate for then,' he says. 'The dressers are from completely different periods, but they coexist so beautifully in the room,' explains Carlos.

Although every element is carefully considered, this is not a museum. Rather, it is a charming, rambling house that proves why taking it slow is one of the best ways to decorate. 'We can get obsessed with everything being super decorated and perfect, but a good interior should put you at ease and bring you joy,' explains Carlos. 'What we wanted to achieve here was a house that felt settled.'

The walls of Carlos's kitchen are painted
in Edward Bulmer's 'Olympian Green', while
the farmhouse table, with legs painted in
'Deep Gres de Flandres Blue' by Papers
and Paints, provides a bit of oomph. Lino
was removed to reveal a floor tiled with
original Norfolk pamments. The enviable
adjoining pantry is filled with open shelves
and baskets for gathering produce.

The downstairs rooms function as an enfilade,
with the dining room – painted in Farrow
& Ball's 'Parma Gray' with a seventeenth-
century oak court cupboard at one end and
chairs in Robert Kime's 'Turkoman Stripe'
– leading onto the drawing room. Walls in
Farrow & Ball's 'Bone' provide a backdrop
to Heriz rugs and a sofa draped in a suzani.

Painted in 'Quaker' by Edward Bulmer,
the guest bedroom plays host to a hand-
carved four-poster Gillows bed decked
out in Carlos's own 'Kandili' fabric. The
curtains are made from the same fabric,
while the chair is upholstered in Robert
Kime's hand-dyed 'Harlequin' ikat.

The bathroom is half in Robert Kime's
'St Abbs' wallpaper and half in Edward
Bulmer's 'Jonquil'. It leads onto an upstairs
hallway that Carlos has painted in a punchy
green – Edward Bulmer's 'Turquoise'. This is
typical of how he likes to use bolder colours in
spaces that you don't linger to create surprise.

AMY BALFOUR

Decorative painter, East Sussex

A few months ago, decorative painter Amy Balfour used an online analysis service to work out what colour clothes most suit her. The verdict? Soft autumn. It makes sense, for hers is a world of rusty reds, mustard yellows, gingers, clay pinks, olives and teals – colours that have punch, but also an earthy richness and understatedness. 'I like warm colours,' says the East Sussex-based artist, who has become known for her beautiful hand-painted creations – everything from intricately decorated doll's houses to Charleston Farmhouse-inspired mirrors and lamps.

Unsurprisingly, this inviting palette also sits at the heart of the fifteenth-century Wealden hall house where she lives with her husband, Victor, and their four – soon to be five – children. And while folk art, vintage fabrics and patterned textiles all play their part in shaping the interiors, it is certain well-deployed colours that really set the tone: the deep mustard on the kitchen cabinets, the olive green on the woodwork in the dining room-cum-entrance hall, and the orangey-pink on the drawing room walls, which bear the textural marks of the brush that applied it. So too do Amy's hand-painted additions, which range from the pretty Bloomsbury-esque detailing that borders the windows and Aga in the kitchen to the yellow sideboard in the playroom, onto which Amy painted a couple of vases of blowsy flowers. 'I don't overthink things,' explains Amy, who often paints in snatched hours around looking after her young children. 'I start painting when I have an idea, and always think that I can just paint over it if it goes wrong,' she says with a smile.

Amy and Victor moved to the house shortly after lockdown. It is the oldest one in the pretty East Sussex village of Fletching, with beautiful rambling gardens that play host to a string of outbuildings that now include Amy's studio. The fact it had been derelict for a couple of years, and had no running water or heating, rudimentary electrics, and crumbling lath and plaster walls did not deter them – in fact, quite the opposite. 'We wanted a proper project,' explains Amy. That, it certainly was, especially when Amy discovered she was expecting triplets, about a month after they had got the keys. It was all hands on deck to get the house into a habitable state. The layout – other than the removal of a secondary staircase – stayed pretty much the same, with a drawing room, dining room, playroom, kitchen and laundry room downstairs, and bedrooms and bathrooms spread across the upper two floors. Victor did everything he could to aid the builders – painting radiators in a little makeshift booth, sanding floors and hanging doors – while Amy, who had spent three years assisting Janie Money at Sibyl Colefax & John Fowler, approached the house like it was a project for a client.

Fittings and paints were ordered, rooms were mapped out, and the budget was cleverly portioned out to ensure that along with the vital but less pretty parts of a renovation – things like stealing a little bit of space from a bedroom to create a more generous family bathroom and lime plastering every wall – there could be a couple of more indulgent flourishes. Wallpapers were chosen for a handful of rooms: St Jude's 'Monkeys and Birds', by Sheila Robinson, (also, incidentally, in George Saumarez Smith's house on pages 46–55) runs amok in the triplets' room, while Edward Bawden's 'Pigeon and Clock Tower' design, also sold through St Jude's, provides a playful backdrop to the downstairs loo. Not only are the papers a tribute to other artists, but the whimsical patterns also seem to speak the same visual language as Amy's work. 'I like things to feel handmade and crafted,' she says. Elsewhere, Amy pattern-rolled a pretty floral motif onto the walls, which gives the look of something between wallpaper and stencilling for a fraction of the price and time. 'My family are all quite creative, and I grew up watching my mum, granny and aunts stamping walls and making their own curtains and rag rugs,' she says. Many of the curtains, such as the Colefax ones in the drawing room and the charming crewelwork ones in the dining room, were sourced second-hand from eBay or Etsy, while others were whipped up from inexpensive fabrics by a good-value curtain maker.

Unlike some of the houses in this book, which have gently evolved over time, this one had a hard and fast deadline. And, somehow, in four and a half months, what was a building site became a colourful and joyful home. Many pieces – such as the Bloomsbury-inspired kitchen table painted by Amy, rugs and the yellow dresser in the playroom – came from their previous home, as did a healthy collection of art that the couple had amassed over the years. 'I love gathering things together to create different layers of texture and pattern,' says Amy. But, as she is quick to admit, when they first moved in,

it seemed like they had only created a framework: 'I felt that it lacked personality and was quite empty,' she explains. Since then, it has gained its layers, and the result is a house that feels – and indeed has been – lovingly collected over time. Some pieces were bought specifically, such as the Hadeda 'Axel' sofa in the drawing room and the beautiful headboard in the main bedroom, which is upholstered in a fabric from Nicholas Herbert. And other bits, such as the beautiful embroidery and lace vintage fabric hanging behind Amy and Victor's bed, have come along the way. 'I go through phases of collecting certain pieces,' Amy explains. 'Currently, it's antique samplers and marquetry pictures.'

Much of its personality comes from Amy's own decorative embellishments, which happen in fits and starts, as time allows. 'I've got great plans to cover just about every surface in painted motifs,' says Amy, who is currently plotting to paint the entrance hall floor. 'It sounds obvious, but every time I paint something, the house feels a little bit more reflective of my style,' she explains. Their bedroom, for instance, really came together after Amy applied a Swedish folk art-inspired floral design in a favourite teal tone to break up the strong red on the existing built-in wardrobes. 'I've always loved Swedish painted furniture and that's part of the reason I became so interested in decorative painting,' explains Amy, whose interest was kick-started by a box-painting class at Charleston Farmhouse with designer and decorative painter Melissa White. Downstairs, in the drawing room, a similar red and teal combination plays out above the fireplace, where Amy has added a simple scallop detail, which gives the peachy-pink room a bit of a punch.

For Amy, decorating and her painting work are alike: 'It's about having confidence in how you put things together, and running with it,' she explains. 'I know what I like and I think it's important to follow your instinct, rather than to try and copy someone else's look.' It's a wise mantra.

A wall of built-in bookshelves, painted in Little Greene's 'Olive', runs the length of the dining room. The fireplace on the opposite wall was already there, with tiles that match the ones in the church opposite the house. Above the oak table hangs Jim Lawrence's 'Barchester Double Pendant Light in Antiqued Brass'.

The DeVol kitchen is painted in Farrow
& Ball's 'India Yellow', while Amy added
the decorative motifs that frame the
Aga and the patterns that border the
doorway. She is also responsible for
the kitchen table, with its Charleston
Farmhouse-inspired top, which came
with the couple from their previous home.

A downstairs loo, papered in St Jude's 'Pigeon and Clock Tower' wallpaper by Edward Bawden, functions as a corridor. One way it leads out into the DeVol kitchen; the other, it goes into the boot room, which is painted in Devol's 'Trinity Blue'. The window curtains in here are made from a Cloth House fabric.

A headboard upholstered in Nicholas
Herbert's 'Bhavani' and a hand-embroidered
grain sack and crochet cloth bought from
Instagram seller Home & Coastal and hung
behind the bed, create a folk feeling in Amy's
bedroom. The wardrobes were hand-painted
by Amy, while the just glimpsed ensuite
bathroom is papered in Anna French's 'Jouy'.
The triplets' bedroom is papered in 'Monkeys
and Birds' by St Jude's.

ABOUT THE AUTHOR

ABOUT THE PHOTOGRAPHER

Elizabeth Metcalfe is a journalist and editor who writes about interiors and design. Having studied English Literature at King's College London and completed an MA in History of Art at the Courtauld Institute of Art, she joined *House & Garden* magazine in 2015, where she is currently the Features Editor. She enjoys writing about houses that are lived-in and layered, as well as discovering craftspeople and houses that are off the beaten track. She lives in West Sussex with her husband, daughter and lurcher.

Dean Hearne is an interiors and portrait photographer based in East Sussex. He has always been fascinated by the power of photography to tell stories, and it was during six months of travelling through the US and Australia in 2000 where his passion really grew. His interest in interiors photography soon followed, and he finds himself particularly drawn to the subtle details that make a home. His clients include *House & Garden*, *Vogue*, Sibyl Colefax & John Fowler and Harrods. He lives in a hilltop village near Hastings with his partner Jeska and their two cats.

ACKNOWLEDGEMENTS

A book is the work of many, many people. Thank you to the whole team at Frances Lincoln – particularly to Anna Watson, my editor, who approached me to write the book and in doing so gave me a bit of confidence in those early days of motherhood; to Charlotte Frost and Isabel Eeles for your wonderful editorial support throughout. I am very grateful to Claire Warner for her brilliant design and for being so tolerant of our suggestions.

Enormous thanks to photographer Dean Hearne, who was a joy to work with and brought a calm presence and fresh eye to every house we visited. It was a bit of a punt when I asked if you would be up for photographing 20 or so houses over the course of a few months, but I am so grateful for your positivity and enthusiasm for what is now very much our book.

But I am perhaps most indebted to the owners of the 22 houses featured, who allowed Dean and me to visit. Without their generosity and huge efforts, none of this would be possible. Photo shoots are intense, long days and although we largely captured spaces as we found them, we are incredibly grateful to everyone's patience as we moved sofas an inch or so, pillaged gardens for greenery and re-organised childrens toys.

Thank you to friends and family for their kindness, encouragement and logistical help. To my parents and parents-in-law, particularly Marian, for helping with childcare at the drop of a hat. I don't think I could have done it without you.

Huge thanks to kind friends who read chapters when I was losing my train of thought.

FInally, to my dear family. To Charlie, for his complete faith that I could write a book four months into maternity leave and for seeing how it would make everything a bit better if I could regain a sense of who I was before we had a baby. If it was not for your encouragement and belief that I could do both, I don't think I'd be writing this. Thank you for always picking up the slack, for being the most amazing father and for bearing with me as I spent evenings and weekends writing. And then to Martha – my wonderful, joyful, adventurous daughter. You and this book have grown alongside one another, and you weren't a bad shoot companion either. You have taught me, more than I could ever imagine, about what truly matters in life.

INDEX

For Charlie

Quarto

First published in 2024 by Frances Lincoln
an imprint of The Quarto Group.
One Triptych Place, London, SE1 9SH
United Kingdom
T (0)20 7700 9000
www.Quarto.com

ISBN 978-0-7112-9334-2
EISBN 978-1-8360-0362-5

10 9 8 7 6 5 4 3 2

Book Design: Claire Warner Studio
Commissioning Editor: Anna Watson
Editorial Director: Nicky Hill
Photographer: Dean Hearne
Publisher: Philip Cooper
Senior Designer: Isabel Eeles
Senior Editor: Charlotte Frost
Production Director: Angela Graef

Printed in China